Widowhood

The Definitive
Turning Point

By Dotty Stephenson

Widowhood - the Definitive Turning Point

Cover design by Adolfo Blanco
Edited by: June Bishop

Library of Congress Cataloging-in-Publication Data
Stephenson, Dotty, 1927-

Widowhood - The Definitive Turning Point / Dotty Stephenson

ISBN: 0-9772160-2-0
1. Widowhood—Religious aspects—Christianity
2. Spiritual life—Christianity

Library of Congress Control Number: 2007922746

"Striking the heart with the Word of God."
A division of Darling, Rose, Joseph, Michaels, & Lee Printing, Publishing, & Communications, LLC
Riverside, CA

In memory of Bill,
My husband, my best friend,
My true soul mate,
and my dearest companion.

Table of Contents

Acknowledgments

Loving thanks to Greg and Cathe Laurie, my Pastor & wife, who gave their gracious support at the time of Bill's death and have continued to do so through all these years.

Thanks to my dear friends Jim & Carol Hoover, Carol for faithful prayers and Jim for locating the "River in the Desert" for me.

Heartfelt thanks to the many who have prayed this book into existence, my Wednesday prayer group, friends from church, Honey, from Washington,

Jan Vance for encouragement, prayers and those all important 'pointers,'

Special thanks to Jan Frank for her love and support and especially her help in pushing me on to expound more, open up more and her prayers – all of it Jan.

Sue, that 'sweet young thing' from up north,

My widows group for their love, prayers and support.

Others too numerous to mention, know that I am so grateful to you for all the prayers.

Scott & Debby Darling, Chris Garner, publishers, editors, helpful beyond measure, multitudes of thanks for having the faith to publish this book.

June Bishop, my wonderful, caring editor.

To our precious children, Debby and John, for being so supportive, not only with the writing of this book, but for the years since Bill left us, thanks always from your 'ever loving' Mom.

Foreword

Widowhood is indeed a definitive turning point in our lives. We are never the same after we lose our spouse—whether we remain single or remarry, our lives are changed forever.

I have discovered there are different phases in widowhood. Acceptance, learning to live as a widow, finding the plan God has that we might be fulfilled once more—these are all steps we struggle through in this bewildering new chapter of our lives.

My prayer for this book is that it will help those of you who are going through the process of learning to live without a husband. This book is not meant to be read through at one sitting. Instead, as your needs and questions arise, look for the section that deals with just that situation. There is a Cover Page for each chapter outlining the difficulties you might be having, and I hope you will find answers to help you.

The fifteenth anniversary of my husband's death is imminent. Through every minute of every day, through all these months and years, the Lord has sustained and strengthened me and He has never left me. He wants to do the same for you. He loves His daughters who are widows so much that we are mentioned by the word widow 49 times in the Bible. Widows are mentioned an additional 24 times, and widowhood is referred to four times.

If you were to take the time to read each of those passages (a concordance will give you the references) you would read of the infinite care He takes and concern He has for each and every widow. Woe to anyone who mistreats us, cheats us, or hurts us in any wrongful way! They will answer to God for what they have done.

He has proven Himself faithful over and over to me and many others. I want to shout from the housetops about what a wonderful, loving God we serve! He tells us in Isaiah 54:5 that He is our husband! And what a mighty husband He is. Who has more wisdom, or more power, or more love, than He does? Our heavenly husband has all this and more.

My theme throughout this book is that He has a new life for us. He knew we would be widows and He made plans for us ahead of time. He wants us to keep our eyes on Him and trust Him, no matter what! I can tell you He will never fail you then—no matter what!

Chapter One

The Dark Nights

"What I tell you in darkness, that speak ye in the light."
Matthew 10:27

In The Dark Nights

"Like a candle lifted in the night
God's love is a light in the darkness."
Anonymous

In Your dark night You saw the brilliance of the
Father's plan. In my dark nights You promised me
the oil of joy for mourning. A garland of beauty
instead of a heavy, burdened, and failing spirit.
Isaiah 61:3

This chapter deals with the pain of grief, the confusion we feel with that soul mate no longer beside us, the bouts we have with depression, loneliness, and learning about aloneness, a new phenomenon for many of us.

It is also the beginning of learning, in a new way, how very great is His faithfulness, and how fathomless are His love and care for those who put their trust in Him.

Dark Night of Grief

The summer was exciting; we were all buzzing with the anticipation of our son's wedding that was to take place in Kauai. Our whole family went and we enjoyed the fun and fellowship of spending time together.

When the wedding was over, my husband Bill and I went to Oahu to visit Pearl Harbor which was having its 50th anniversary. Bill was a veteran of WWII and we very much wanted to visit the USS Arizona Memorial. It was a heart-wrenching experience to stand there above the Arizona and remember the 2390 lives that were lost on that day of infamy. We bought a souvenir to take home with us; little realizing that I would soon be using it in a service memorial to commemorate Bill's military service in the Navy.

Leaving Hawaii, we flew home for a week and then took off for our annual August trek to Baja, California. We were staying three weeks and had friends coming down during this time. Bill played golf with his buddies two and three times every week while we gals shopped and visited.

Tuesday morning of the third week everyone had left and we were alone. When Bill got up, he didn't feel well and went back to bed. That was my last full day with my husband.

Noon rolled around and I knew Bill wasn't getting any better: he wouldn't consider seeing a doctor there in Baja so I began packing our car for the trip home. All the while Bill kept saying he would be better, to wait.

Finally he realized he wasn't getting better. He was so weak by this time I had to have the guards at the gate help me get him into the car. We rushed back home arriving at the Riverside hospital at 1:00 a.m. By 6:00 a.m. Bill had slipped from this life into eternity with his Lord.

There was no warning, there had been no prior sickness, and yet, in a day my husband was gone. I have heard the definition of death as total and final cessation of all vital functions. One thing is certain, whether our spouses have had a long lingering illness, or are taken quickly, death is final.

I marveled at the way the Lord was so infinitely kind and loving. He took the terrible pain and despair I was feeling and wrapped it in a divine anesthetic. It was like being in a cocoon of love.

He even gave me clarity of mind for all the important and necessary decisions that had to be made at that time. I had to decide about such things as clothes, shoes, and accessories that must be delivered to the mortuary; songs to be sung; favorite scripture verses—all those things that were special to Bill, things unbearable to think of without the Lord's help. I have heard other widows speak of this time and how the Lord seemed to cover every necessity with His peace and love.

I was so blessed with all that my church and my friends did to help. Their love, support and just being there for me and our children was wonderful. I encourage every widow I meet, if she is not already in a church fellowship, to get in one. There is such strength and comfort for the family in being surrounded with fellow believers.

A month or two into widowhood, I noticed the Lord withdrawing His divine anesthetic by degrees: so much after one month, so much more at two months, and so forth. Finally, I was finding the strength to stand on my own. I was also aware that He was always there, offering His support for each day, just as He promised. "…I will never, no never, no never leave you or forsake you…" (See Hebrews 13:5). And He never has.

The incredible pain of that first year made me think my body was one long incision, as if half of me had been wrenched away. I had trouble walking, as if I couldn't find my balance with half of me gone. I wondered what the Lord would do with all this pain. Even as I meditated on the answer, I knew it depended on me. It was my choice whether or not I would let the Lord heal my grief. I could choose to hug the pain to myself and perhaps become a bitter, lonely and resentful person. Or I could turn it over to the Lord and ask Him to bring good out of all this as He promised to do. (See Romans 8:28.) If I chose to believe Him and claim His promises, He would then be free to give me the oil of joy for mourning and the garland of beauty instead of the heavy, burdened and failing spirit I was experiencing. (See Isaiah 61:3.)

There is no way to explain grief. It is like a fellowship, those who have similar experiences are members. It made me think of when I became a grandmother for the first time. Only those who were grandmothers truly knew what it was like. Those who have never experienced grief can never know what it is like. I thought of what agony God must have endured watching His son die. The pain of my grief immobilized me, shattered me.

I knew I was being allowed a tiny glimpse of what it cost my Father to send His Son to the cross for all mankind.

When grief overpowered me I would just say His name, 'Jesus', 'Jesus'. During one of these times the Lord had a friend call me who has a beautiful voice. She said, "The Lord has told me to call and sing a love song to you." I wept, feeling the magnitude of the love He has for all His children. I knew the comfort that I was experiencing was the same comfort He extended to all who were in great suffering. He wants to wrap us in His tender mercy and experience His loving-kindness, unending and unsurpassed for sheer grace, just as He promised. He wants us to discover the sweetness of His fellowship, the steadfastness of His promises, and the strength of His mighty power.

Dark Night of Confusion

I was confused, baffled, and bewildered, and having a hard time getting my life into balance. In other words, I was trying to discover what I was to do with my life! I wanted the Lord to write on the wall of my house clear directions for me as He had written on the wall warning King Belshazzar (see Daniel 5:5).

I certainly didn't want a writing of judgment like He sent Belshazzar. I wanted the Lord to coddle me, take my hand and help me find those easy pathways. Couldn't He see all my confusion? I wanted clear understanding of what I was to do now that I no longer had a husband. I could almost hear Him say, "And if I do all of that, daughter, how will you build your faith in Me?"

Reading Psalm 71, I saw that David cried out for the Lord to deliver him, rescue him. He said he had put his trust in the Lord, who was his hope, his rock. I knew I was to have the same heart attitude as David. So I cried out and said, "Lord! Give me a heart like David's."

I already knew that when I obey the Lord and take one day at a time, He will guide me. He is my refuge, my strength. I knew I could confidently put my trust in Him. So why did I have such a hard time doing this? I think I ran off in all directions and stayed confused as I felt overwhelmed with the enormity of life without my beloved husband. Who was I going to talk things over with, who would help me make the right decisions that need to be made almost daily?

I knew I had to choose either confusion or the Lord's plan for me, as He will not violate our free will. I was exhausted with running here and there seeking a husband who was no longer in my life. I said, "Okay, Lord, take my hand and guide me into this new life. In myself I can't make it, but You are not a God of confusion but of peace and order" (See 1 Corinthians 14:33).

Dark Night of Aloneness

I discovered there was another hill to climb in that first year. It was learning the difference between being lonely and aloneness. Unless you have experienced aloneness you might think the difference is simply a matter of semantics. But it is far more.

Loneliness after the loss of a husband makes one feel isolated and this solitude can lead to wanting to live in seclusion.

When this happens, such heaviness of grief invades that jumping in a black pit and covering your head sounds good.

Aloneness is being so very aware that the other half of you is gone. The one you went out to dinner with, the trips you made together, the projects you worked on, the goals you reached, like painting a room together—that husband is no longer there to do all these things and more with you. You are alone. That is different from loneliness. You are so very aware that you are not two any longer, you are just one.

When loneliness gripped me I would get in a funk, and when aloneness surrounded me I would become angry, usually at Bill, as if he had a choice in leaving me down here all alone! While doing my hair one morning I thought of how much I missed my husband. When he used the bathroom I would grumble about the water splashed all over, the mirror messed up, and the sink needing cleaning. Now when I walk in, it is neat and clean and I am jolted into the awareness that I am alone!

Holidays of any kind are hard to endure. I remember going to my local market at Christmastime and as I walked through the door I was immediately surrounded by happy, chattering people. Almost everyone had a mate to talk and laugh with while I was submerged in my aloneness. I was surprised at the anger that surged through me. How dare these people be so happy when I was alone! My pain was so deep it was hard to breathe. I hurried back to the car so that my tears could be released in privacy.

I dreaded going home to an empty house. Consequently I was with friends as much as possible. When I was at home, I turned the radio on as soon as I walked in the door. I needed to hear a voice filling the void. Having a desperate need to be with others I had shut out His still, small voice. I knew my husband wasn't coming back, but I was not ready to embrace a new life apart from the one I had had with a man I dearly loved.

One day I seemed to hear the Lord say to me, "You enjoy the company of others more than mine." I thought, it's true, I do. I wasn't aware that I was taking anything away from my dependence on the Lord by doing this. He didn't agree with me and wanted to show me the difference between walking in victory and experiencing defeat in my aloneness.

The Lord was dealing with me on two levels. First, I needed to accept the fact that my husband was dead and to quit living in the past. Second, I needed to accept by faith the new life He had already prepared for me (See Psalm 139:16).

Meditating on His sovereignty helped me to remember that nothing comes to me except through His loving hands. Therefore, if He chose for me to become a widow at this time of my life, then that is the very best plan His great love has for me. Whatever I need, He is more than able to provide. I recognized it was a matter of trust. His Word tells me the paths I am to walk were prepared ahead of time (See Ephesians 2:10). Acknowledging the truth of His foreknowledge, I realized once more that He wasn't surprised at my being a widow - I was.

He brought to my remembrance what He had said about never leaving me or forsaking me (see Hebrews 13:5). Couldn't I trust a God who could love me that much and believe Him to take away my pain of aloneness?

Of course I could; after all, He promised that His presence would be with me always. Again, it was a choice. I could choose to live in despair or choose to walk in His strength knowing He could take all that pain and bring good out of it. How? I didn't know, but He did. I trusted Him to take this terrible aloneness from me. He was free to bring about His plan for my life.

Dark Night of Depression

That first year of dark nights brought with it the battle against depression. The dictionary says depression is "the state of being depressed in spirits; dejection; a low state of strength." Yes! All of the above described me at various times. I didn't like being a widow and I struggled so hard to accept God's will for my life. I enjoyed being with people but I discovered that depression set in when I was alone again (I learned later that this happens to most widows). I would read a book to escape my own thoughts and run across incidents that reminded me of my husband. Sorrow and tears would engulf me. I never knew what would trigger a new battle with the dreaded malady of depression.

I analyzed different circumstances and how I reacted inwardly to them. Doing this made me realize that there were only two groups of people I was secure with: my own personal family and my close inner-family at church. Being with any one else brought on terrible feelings of insecurity; I was so aware of feeling like half a person without Bill.

The Bible is always God's answer, so I looked closely at Isaiah 54:4-5. In that passage, He said I was not to fear, nor to be ashamed, confounded, or depressed, because He was my husband. Then He explained what an awesome husband He is. He was my Maker, He created me. That meant He knew every single thing about me. He understood my thinking, the reason why I do things the way I do. Therefore, I could trust Him to know the very best way to make my life worthwhile again. Hope began to overcome depression.

He said the Lord of hosts was His name. That meant there was no enemy that He hadn't conquered. When I placed my faith in Him I was invincible. Peace began to fill me.

Then He said that the Holy One of Israel was my Redeemer. I saw His *agape* love for me. I remembered the price He paid on the cross to redeem me and His love began swallowing up the last dredges of depression.

Finally, He said that He is my husband and emphatically stated that He is God of the whole earth. That covers everything, everywhere! Wherever I might be, with friends or alone, if I felt like half a person and insecure, it meant I was letting depression fog up my perspective of who I was to Him and all He is to me. I thought of the book, '*The Practice of the Presence of God*,' by Brother Lawrence. Instead of dwelling on how alone I was, I needed to exercise my faith and concentrate on His presence with me.

Sometimes I could almost hear Him sigh with relief as I learned these hard lessons. He wanted me to grasp what He already knew, that when I trust Him with my whole heart, fear and depression have to flee! The Lord would show me these new areas of life where my faith and trust in Him were essential if I was to walk in the freedom He had for me. I had to choose to grasp the truth of what He was telling me and labor until I had entered into that truth (see Hebrews 4:11).

I don't want anyone to think that I would see where I needed to build more trust in Him, believe Him, and blink, the light would go on! No, it was one step at a time, each day working to find that path free of pain that I knew He had for me. Grief is a process and if there is a short-cut to get through it I never saw it. Linking up by faith with my heavenly husband means His light illuminates every dark corner of my paths. As black and depleting as depression is, when my eyes are on Jesus, the Light of the world, depression is swallowed up in His great victory for all His children.

Dark Night of Learning Contentment

A year passed before I allowed the word widow to enter into my vocabulary. It was too painful, unthinkable, and unbearable – how could this be?

Many years before my husband died I discovered the 54th chapter of Isaiah. I thought then that it was the most beautiful love letter to widows in the whole Bible. After Bill's death, I began to read it in earnest. In the fifth verse the Lord says, "For your Maker is your husband…". Reading it this time I noticed He didn't say, "Make Me your husband." He said, "Your Maker is your husband." I had never realized before that there were no options.

I then discovered the fact that knowing something with my mind did not necessarily mean I knew it with my heart. I was amazed at the resistance within me to accept the Lord as my heavenly husband. How could I exchange the earthly for the heavenly?

A little over a year after Bill died, I was sitting in church one Sunday before the service began when a dear friend approached me. His eyes full of compassion as he asked, "How are you doing?" I replied, "Pretty good, how about you?" The past year and the many prayers we had prayed for each other flashed through my mind. My friend's big battle was job related. Mine was struggling with this new life brought about by the death of my husband.

With a sigh my friend said, "The Lord seems to be speaking one word to me, 'Contentment'." I burst into tears as a huge light of revelation flooded my mind and heart. God knew the turmoil going on inside of me was terrible. I missed my husband; I wanted him sharing my life again. Resisting being alone was a fierce battle and the Lord was using my friend to get His message though to me. God had been nudging me for over a year to accept my new life as a widow and to trust Him and His plan for my life. I wanted to obey but didn't know what was blocking my acceptance of His will. Greatly concerned because of the torrential tears, my friend said, "We just want to minister to you." I was laughing and crying by this time. "You have ministered to me. *Contentment* is what God has been asking me to enter into for over a year."

Finally, I understood where the block had been. The Lord knew that contentment was a word that had not entered my mind since my husband's death. I was still crying, but with tears of cleansing, of refreshing and acceptance of what my heavenly Father was asking of me—to be content with His plan (See Philippians 4:11).

The Lord understood I wasn't rejecting Him as my heavenly husband, I had been rejecting the fact that I no longer had an earthly husband. Being content in my widowhood meant I accepted God's will for my life; it meant I trusted Him for His plan for my life (see Ephesians 2:10). I marvel constantly that we serve a God who will not let us settle for defeat, but insists on nudging us on into the victory His Son won for us on the cross.

I remember saying to the Lord at this time, "Okay, Lord, I choose to be content as a widow, but Lord, use me, don't leave me down here to spin my wheels. If You are not going to use me, take me home now!" Even now, after fifteen years of widowhood, struggling, resisting, pondering each new area the Lord was moving me into, I marvel at how the Lord hasn't said to me, "Swat! You're out of here." But He never has and He keeps my plate just right, not too full and never empty. I am so grateful for the gift of 'contentment.' He is so patient and full of loving understanding with each one of us, beyond any doubt we can trust Him for our new life.

Seeing God's Purpose in the Dark Night

The Bible tells us that though the mountains should depart and the hills be shaken or removed, yet His love and kindness shall not depart from us (see Isaiah 54:10). When we are widows, the mountains of security, of normalcy, of companionship have departed from us. Our hills of flesh-and-blood spouses to talk to, to share with, to walk into old age with, have been removed.

Originally I could not think about all this for too long at a time, it was too horrible to comprehend. That is when the Lord would swoop down, enfold me in His arms, and shower me with His love and kindness. He had been through the agony of losing that One dearest to His heart. He knew how to comfort and encourage.

I remembered that we are told His light would dispel the darkness of this world (see John 1:5). I needed Jesus to dispel the darkness that had enfolded my world, and He did. There were times when Satan would try to come in and shroud me with darkness again. And in that darkness, self-pity (which is vicious) would clamor for entrance. Sometimes I would let it in. It always felt so good to just sink down and wallow in darkness. When this happened, I would lose contact with my Lord. My faith would be like fluttering little wings with not enough strength to fly up and make connection with His mighty power. That is when His covenant of peace and completeness would invade and His love and kindness would begin to edge out despair and hopelessness.

I felt fragmented but He was ever in the process of completing me. Seeing Him shine His light into my dark nights caused my faith to grow, my hope to rise, and my peace to prevail. Finally, I saw that the Lord was using all this to reveal Himself to me in new and deeper ways than I would ever have known otherwise.

I want to encourage others who have lost their loved ones. God is no respecter of persons; His promises and love are for all His children. The Lord has never failed me in the many years that I have been a widow. There have been valleys of despair, mountains of decisions, battles of grief and pain, yet, through it all, He faithfully meets my every need and keeps His every promise.

During the dark night of parting from my husband the Lord was my support and strength. When I wanted to sink into oblivion He was there nudging, urging, and encouraging me to the place He had planned for me in the land of the living. He has paths planned for us to walk in, and He has good works foreordained for us to do (see Ephesians 2:10). Isn't that a marvelous promise? All He asks of us is to believe Him and trust Him to do all He has said.

Is that easy to do? No. It takes an act of will to choose His way, His plan for my life. Some days I woke up saying, "Oh Lord, thank You for this new life You have given me." Other mornings I would awake saying, "Oh Lord, I can't make it but please don't leave me." Sometimes He would leave me in my misery and self-pity until I realized, "O God, this isn't where I want to live!" I firmly accepted my widowhood, after much agonizing, as a fact of life and said, "Yes, Lord, I choose that new life You have planned for me." Only another widow knows how hard it is to relinquish the life she has known with her husband, and choose the totally unknown. Unless we do that the Lord is not free to begin to work out His plan and purpose for our lives.

It is so important to *know* Him and know of His great love for us. When we do, *then* we can trust Him with our whole heart for that new life.

God's Promises, God's Power
Our Choice

Grief brings to our hearts and minds confusion, depression, discontentment, and many other different emotions. We must remember that God has the answers to our every dilemma.

❖ We do not serve a God of confusion; He has a clear path planned for us. Our part is to ignore the fog we are in and *trust Him* to keep our feet from going to the left or to the right.

❖ Depression is a vicious culprit; another tactic of the enemy to keep us from the peace our Lord has given us. We must learn to refuse to give up that peace and by His power within us we claim it *by faith* as ours.

❖ Choosing contentment in our present circumstances as a widow is an act of the will. We do this by telling the Lord we *believe Him* to take the incredible pain of our loss and cover it with His love.

Chapter Two

In The Winepress

"Out of the presses of pain
Cometh the soul's best wine,
The eyes that have shed no rain.
Can shed but little shine."
A.B. Simpson

In The Winepress

"I have held many things in my hand, and I have lost them all; but whatever I have placed in God's hands, that I shall possess."
Martin Luther

Your winepress, O Lord, is used to remove every vestige of self. When my rights are laid at the Cross and Your will becomes my consuming desire, You lift the pressure and can then use me as poured out wine.

There is life after the death of a spouse. When the initial shock has worn off and the pain of missing that loved one has become intermittent instead of continual, we have a choice to make. God has a plan for our lives but we have to choose that life and know it is for our very best.

The winepress in Biblical days was a trough; usually of stone. The grapes were pressed by men treading them, holding to ropes suspended overhead. The juice flowed through a hole near the bottom into a vat.

The winepress in the picture at the front of this chapter used a heavy cylinder which was lowered by pulling the lever on the right side of the vat which pressed the juice from the grapes. Today, many wineries have huge metal tanks and much of the juice extraction process is mechanized.

The symbolism of the winepress is what I wish to use in this chapter. When we feel pressed beyond measure we are like those grapes that are pressed until there isn't a drop of moisture left in them. God is using great pressure in our lives to mold us into that person who will become poured-out wine for others and for Him.

The Winepress

I consider myself an amateur photographer and was always interested in capturing pictures that could later be used in a pictorial devotional that I was putting together. I wanted a picture of an old winepress, but didn't know how to go about finding one. When I took my problem to my husband, Bill, he simply said, "Use the phone book and call the wineries and see if they have an old winepress."

Lo and behold I found one! Bill was always willing to help me "catch" the right pictures, so we planned a Saturday when he would not be working, took a picnic and set off to find the old winepress. I never dreamed that one day I would be using that same picture to illustrate how the pressure of my grieving for Bill made me feel like I was in a winepress. I wasn't sure of just what it was the Lord wanted to extract from me, but at times it felt like *everything*!

I knew my life was changed forever; being a widow certainly is a definitive turning point. The Lord was continually nudging me to accept the *fact* that I was a widow. Bill was gone, and my perspective regarding my life had to change.

For instance, one time when coming home from a trip to Arizona, I felt as if I were back in the winepress as a new thought occurred to me. Driving down Cajon Pass, (a very steep and long grade you must go through when coming from the High Desert of California back into San Bernardino,) the thought popped into my mind. I would grow old alone; Bill would not grow old along with me! I shrank from the thought of facing the future alone. Pain pierced through me and tears streamed down my face. I couldn't see to drive and I wondered if I might not be joining Bill sooner than I thought, as Cajon Pass is not a place to drive with blurred vision. I said, "Lord! You have to help me. Strengthen me and dry up these tears." He did and I could see to drive again, but the pain of accepting this new truth was ricocheting around in my mind even as I tried to block out the unbelievable thought.

When I got home my prayer was for Him to reconcile this new truth in my heart, help me to understand how I was to have peace once more. He seemed to whisper so sweetly, "I am your husband now, (see Isaiah 54:5) and I will never, no never, no never, leave you or forsake you…" (see Hebrews 13:5).

Did I just latch on to these truths at once and walk in victory and peace? No, but I did *choose* to accept His promises and asked that they be made real in my life. It is one day at a time, and one step at a time. I can truthfully say that when I stumble or falter He is always there to strengthen me, or encourage me—sometimes through people, sometimes through a note in the mail or perhaps through something written in a book.

The Lord was showing me, through the experiences of the winepress, that in a small way I was being allowed to enter into the fellowship of His sufferings *if* I would submit to His hand applying the pressure. His purpose for the pressure in my life is to extract the selfishness, the self-centeredness, and learn to put my trust in Him.

My selfishness and self-centeredness caused me to dwell on *my* needs, *my* hurts. This caused me to be consumed with my problems such as the watering system that was watering the street more than my lawn and the air conditioner that was making unusual loud noises. My refrigerator was freezing things on the refrigerator side not just the freezer side, etc. Obviously I had to see that these things were taken care of, but I didn't have to settle down into gloom because of them.

The Lord's remedy was to get me interested in helping others; go see that person, write that note or make that phone call. I found that baking nut bread to take to someone was always very much appreciated. (And it made me feel good to make someone else feel good!) I found the more I was involved with others; the less time I had for self-pity or depression! And the amazing thing was how the Lord brought just the right help to fix the air conditioning, the watering system, the refrigerator. Naturally He knew He was going to do all that for me but He couldn't do anything as long as I continued to wallow around in self-pity and misery.

Looking back on those years, I see how wise the Lord is and how very patient He is with me—and above all how necessary the wine-press was and is in my life.

Perpetual Pain

All widows do not have the same experiences; there isn't a formula for walking through the process of grief because we are all different. Many of us endure excruciating pain in those early years. My experience made me think of Jeremiah crying out to the Lord about his perpetual pain (Jeremiah 15:18). That's how I felt—the pain of missing Bill seemed to be perpetual.

Staying busy was essential to me, as I would concentrate on the goal to be reached and try not to think about this wounded body that was without the other half of me. I decided to wash my windows. Bill and I had a routine, he did the outside of the windows and I did the inside. The outside needed doing and Bill wasn't here, so that left me. Climbing up on the step-ladder I scrubbed away, and as I reached for the paper towels to dry the window I fell. I lay there a minute checking to see if I had broken anything. Then I became embarrassed for fear someone would see me and rushed into the house bursting into copious tears. I was fine except for a few bruises and lots of self-pity! I told the Lord how unfair it seemed not having my husband to help me. How was I supposed to keep my windows clean?

I wouldn't have any repairman in my house that I or my children didn't know; certainly not a window cleaner. After all they might have ulterior motives, such as coming back and robbing me! I saw the goodness of the Lord later that day when He had my son call me. I told him what had happened and asked, "What in the world am I going to do?" He had used a window cleaner for years and said, "Mom, you will love his work and he is honest as the day is long." The cleaner was everything my son had said, so that problem was solved. The Bible says, "…if you return (give up this mistaken tone of distrust and despair), then I will give you again a settled place of quiet and safety…" (see Jeremiah 15:19).

I was back in the winepress again and the Lord wanted every vestige of fear out of my life. Fear about the different workman needed to help me keep the house and yard together. Fear about the future, fear of all the questions of the unknown, and they were legion. But where there is fear there is no faith. I knew He was asking me to refuse all the fear and trust Him, to change my attitude to one of acceptance of His plan for me. Hadn't I already done this by being "content in whatever my circumstances…" (Philippians 4:11)?

I thought of the winepress and how the skins are stripped to release the grape juice. God wanted to strip my unbelief from me, which was vile in His sight, and fill me with faith. It was then I understood that acceptance of His plan would need to be made daily. My despair was blatant unbelief in His ability to comfort and care for me. His Word convicted me and I asked His help in trusting and accepting His plan for my life once more.

He encouraged me further by promising He would be with me, as He had been with Jeremiah. God promised to make Jeremiah a fortified, brazen wall (see Jeremiah 15:20). I liked that; that was the kind of strength I needed. My enemies were not people, as Jeremiah's were. Mine were spirits of despair, self-pity, pain, discouragement and hopelessness, but I needed the Lord to deliver me, just as much as Jeremiah had needed deliverance.

One of my biggest problems (and this caused big heartache as well) was not having Bill to talk with, to help me make decisions. If I talked to my children about replacing this, or buying that, they would say, "Mom, go ahead do what you want to about that situation." That wasn't what I wanted at all. I wanted Bill there so we could discuss, "Can we afford this?" "Is this the right time to replace so and so?" It took a while, but finally I began to understand that the Lord didn't want me running to anyone for advice, He wanted me coming to Him, my heavenly husband! He was all wise and all knowing and was all I would ever need.

Did I make mistakes? You bet I did, every time I ran ahead of Him and decided I could take care of this on my own (like taking my car to my car dealer instead of asking Him who I should ta. to.)

I felt like He was cleaning the windows of my soul by washing away the layers of grief and pain and I was getting a much clearer insight into His plans of quiet and safety for me. He enabled me by His love to loose my feelings of desolation to Him and to experience the beginning invasion of quiet and safety He promised me.

I could not help but thank Him for holding me close (that's when the squeezing takes place), drying my tears, and causing me once more to see how foolish I am when I don't put all my trust in Him.

Relinquishing Resistance

Even though I was praying, "Jesus, please don't let me miss You," resistance to His plan for my life was ruling and reigning. He was God and all knowing, but I felt He had made a very large mistake in making me a widow! I didn't verbalize that He had made a mistake and didn't allow myself to admit I was even thinking such a thing. My resistance was passive. I would not accept the fact that His plan for my life was for good and not evil. The Lord compelled and constrained me in my winepress. He let me strain and struggle as I fought acceptance of the fact that my life was changed forever. I was running here and there searching for the one I had lost, knowing I could never find him.

I have read in the Bible where someone said, "And he came to himself." That is how I felt when one day I thought, *what is the matter with me, to allow myself to flounder in such an endless sinkhole*? I found out that is the way self-pity works. You keep sinking down into this black hole and finally convince yourself it feels so good, and you think you will stay there!

Years before, I had stood with my husband on the hill of Gethsemane in Israel. I remembered uncontrollable tears pouring from my eyes as I thought of how greatly the Lord had suffered for me. Jesus never uttered one word of complaint, He simply set His face like flint and obeyed His Father's will. My thoughts were once more on the example He had set for me to follow. Once more His infinite love was drawing me back to the land of the living.

The Lord had not asked me to hang on a cross, He had asked me to trust Him in this new chapter of my life. I hadn't done too well with saying, "Okay, Lord, let's get this new life moving right along." So far, I seemed to balk at every step; He just kept nudging me to trust and obey. I needed to confess the sin of resisting His will. It is hard to yield to the squeezing that must take place if that new life is to come forth, but He caused me to remember that He hadn't made a mistake yet, therefore, I could indeed trust Him. I marvel at His patience and love for me. He knows that even though the squeezing is necessary, it is never pleasant. Oswald Chamber says, "We want to be that poured out wine, but we don't like the fingers that do the squeezing."

The Lord waits patiently as I struggle with these new concepts of life without my husband. I struggle to believe He really does have a new life for me as a single woman. I struggle with fear at the reality that Bill isn't here, and that I now face the huge responsibility of making decisions on my own. But the squeezing was teaching me to listen quietly to that still, small voice as He taught me to trust Him with every decision, with every obstacle, with every question.

And slowly He was taking that perpetual pain and making me stronger in my faith, and in my love and trust for Him.

Squeezed into Trusting

The loud thud against my bedroom wall in the early morning hours woke me with a jarring start. My heart hammered with fear, even as I groaned with exhaustion at the awareness of more harassment.   "Lord," I cried, "I am so weary of these frightful experiences that seem to go on and on since my husband died, even to my house being vandalized. Please give me understanding of what You are trying to teach me." Silence greeted my quaking pleas. I called my son the next morning and asked what could be done to increase the security I already had. Choosing among several options, we set the next day for installation of even more motion detector lights.

That evening my fear progressed right along with the ever-lengthening shadows of the setting sun. It was terrible. I remembered God's promise of peace from fear: "You shall establish yourself on righteousness, in conformity with God's will and order; you shall be far even from the thought of oppression or destruction, for you shall not fear; and from terror, for it shall not come near you" (see Isaiah 54:14 Amplified Bible).

Well, I did have fear, and terror flooded me during the dark night hours. That little phrase, "…conformity to God's will and order…" mystified me and I didn't have peace about it, but didn't know where I wasn't conforming. Asking for the Lord's protection, I went to bed about 10:00 pm and struggled to overcome fear as every muscle and nerve was pulled tight. I read until 11:00 pm and turned the light out. There were more noises and bumps in the night than ever. When midnight came, I got up and turned the floodlights on; I saw nothing, turned them off and went back to bed to read some more. There was very little sleep that night as fear clutched me like a vise. When 4:30 a.m. arrived, that still, small voice spoke to me. "Cursed is the man who trusts in the Arm of the flesh but blessed is the man who trusts in the Lord." (Jeremiah 17:5)

Suddenly I realized that each time the attacks started there was another round of beefing up security. My trust was in the flesh (that is in the motion lights, flood lights and alarms) not in the Lord! I called my son at 6:45 a.m. and cancelled any further security plans. When I hung up the phone not only peace, but freedom from all fear flooded me and the Lord filled me with His joy. I understood that conforming to God's will and order was refusing to trust in the arm of the flesh. He wanted me to stop increasing the ample security I already had. He is my security and the One in whom I place my confidence. There was no need for more of man's efforts.

Not all women go through this kind of fear when they are living alone, but I did. The Lord was teaching me trust in every area of my life. He was in total control and if there really were someone outside my house, He has promised to fight for me (see 2 Chronicles 20:15). Did I believe Him? My trust and confidence grew through the months, until at last I could say, "…blessed is the *woman* who trusts in the Lord…" (see Psalm 34:8), and sleep through the night.

I'm so glad the Lord doesn't mind our taking baby steps. What He doesn't want is blatant unbelief in His promises. I have read about that leap of faith, but I had seldom experienced it in all these new lessons He was teaching me. There are over 5000 promises from God in the Bible. While I was learning to have absolute faith in His promises, my steps were faltering, floundering, or failing. I am amazed continually at His patience and compassion towards me

I also see the need for the winepress. Without the pressures of these trials, I would just stay in failure and never become that poured-out wine that glorifies Him.

My Rights

There was another area of struggling where I felt the squeezing of the winepress. There were so many changes in my life and decisions to be made (with no husband to help) and I was having trouble turning to the Lord for His direction in these things. I went through mega mental gymnastics while wrestling with God and His plan for my life, plus the bewilderment of facing a total change of order which left me with lots of questions.

He made me a widow; I didn't ask to be one. My will had to bow to His sovereignty and my heart had to trust in Him. Was He aware that with my husband gone, I lost the joys of partnership:

shared responsibilities, shared plans and fellowship? Who was I going to talk to about all these decisions, problems, and directions that needed attention? (I know I've mentioned this before but it was a big problem in my new life.)

God knew I was trying to find my way being a widow mentally and emotionally. There was no question about the physical fact: I wasn't given an option, my husband was gone. I was learning I didn't have options mentally or emotionally either. To me it seemed that in the eyes of the world, the change of status from being married to being single was going from first class to second class citizen. I felt I didn't fit anywhere.

All these questions were creating unbearable pressures within me; I finally realized (again) the Lord's purpose in all this was to teach me to trust Him for every decision. The Lord helped me remember that He had left the throne of glory and shed all His divine rights to become a Savior to the world. That made me realize that the important fact about my status was not that I was single, but how I chose to *receive* this change in my life.

I meditated on that fact and thought of how the Lord led a single life while He was on this earth, so that He might become the Bridegroom of the church. Furthermore, when I became a widow, He declared Himself my husband (see Isaiah 54:5) He filled that 54th chapter of Isaiah with glorious promises for me if I would choose to avail myself of them.

He reminded me that the only question He asked His Father was, *What would You have Me to say or do?* Then He set about to carry out His Father's will. That's what He was asking of me, to choose my Father's will and trust Him for the plan He had for my life. I wanted the Lord to use me and I remembered how I had said to Him after Bill died, "Lord, either use me or take me home…"

It was nonsense to resist Him. He was offering something so much better than the confusion and bewilderment I was experiencing. I thought of how the skin is slipped off the grape when pressure is applied. I also felt my resistance slipping away, so His purpose could be fulfilled in my life. I could yield to the pressure of His hand, accepting His will for my life, and enter into the joy of knowing that He had a greater plan than self-indulged misery. I knew other Christians who were in far worse trials and yet all of us were putting one foot forward after another, laboring to reach the goal the Lord had set for us. I was blessed with wonderful memories of a loving husband. I knew Bill and I would share eternity together as we are not as those without hope.

When I looked back at how I had clung to what I thought of as my rights, I asked for His forgiveness. His plan for my life is so much larger than anything I could ever imagine. He was asking that I trust Him as the Guardian of my vineyard and not resist the pressure, the pain, the pruning that was necessary to become that empty vessel that He might fill with Himself to be used to bring glory to Him.

Tending My Vineyard

A verse from Song of Solomon 2:15 came to mind as I meditated on my vineyard (life): "…Take us the foxes, the little foxes that spoil the vineyards (of our love), for our vineyards are in blossom." Foxes are known to be sly and cunning, and that is how they gain entrance into our lives. They slink around until a chink in our armor is revealed and then they pounce!

I thought of the chinks I had allowed in my life's armor. One chink was worrying over my finances instead of trusting the Lord. Another was feeling overwhelmed with the care and responsibility of car, house and yard, as though God wasn't able to supply my needs, or bring the right person to help. My most consistent chink wanted to bury my head like an ostrich, instead of getting on with the plan the Lord had for my life. This truly was spoiling the blossoms of our love. Once again, fear was the culprit and my Lord was asking that I trust Him with my life.

I was learning how deadly the little foxes were. I saw they were the annoyances, cares and problems of life used to destroy my relationship with the Lord. They also caused me to ignore the checks that the Holy Spirit would give me as warnings.

For instance, I wanted to visit a place my husband and I had enjoyed immensely. I felt God telling me not to go, but I chose to ignore the warning and went ahead. When I arrived it was terrible; the reality that Bill was not there and would never be there crushed me with despair. I drove home in tears. Careless tending of my vineyard resulted in the sin of disobedience, this brought depression and I missed having sweet fellowship with the Lord that I sorely needed.

I realized how much the foxes used the self-life life to keep me from listening for His guidance. I kept hearing them say "Go ahead, do what you want" in my mind. That was much easier to do than denying myself, wasn't it? Not really. Eventually it dawned on me that I had lost the sense of His presence, my peace was gone and confusion reigned. During this time I remembered that the Lord said if I would abide in Him, He would abide in me and I would bear much fruit (see John chapter 15). I hadn't thought of checking my fruit crop lately but when I did it was very skimpy, practically non-existent. How was the Lord going to have all those vats of wine from such a skimpy crop?

Those annoying little foxes will always be slinking around trying to steal my love, joy and peace. What is my Guardian teaching me through all this? The main thing is to stay close to Him so that when He whispers, I can hear Him. We all know that verse, "Be still and know that I am God" (Psalm 46:10). I can keep my body still, but keeping my mind still is a labor when it is full of thoughts like doubt, fear, anxiety, and worry about tomorrow. I have learned that *being still* is an ongoing lesson, it takes discipline, and it's imperative that I obey. Why? Because every day I need to hear from Him on what His plan is, not only for my life but for others that He has placed in my path.

The wonderful thing about the Lord is that when those sly little devil foxes come around, you and I can lean on His bosom like John did, and say, "Okay, Beloved Guardian, here they come

again, chase them away so that my vines are not spoiled anymore!"
Gazing around this new vineyard where He has planted me, my
dearest hope is that when the Guardian of the vineyard comes to in-
spect the crop it will be healthy and abundant! And this time when
the pressure begins I will feel the love in the fingers that are squeezing and not the pain.

Poured Out for Him

If there is a desire in our hearts to be broken bread and
poured out wine, to be used by our Lord for others, it is our Lord
who chooses the method of squeezing. The time and the place are
in His hands. We have no say in the matter.
I look back with amazement on that first year of widowhood. Now
I understand the Lord was squeezing out the self-life life that was
constantly hindering His plans for my life. Mentally, physically,
and emotionally I was worn out. But spiritually He caused me to
abound in my growth of faith in Him. That's what the trials and
tribulations are all about, teaching us to grow up in Him.

I learned I was so weak I could not stand or walk except
when I clung to Him and let His strength fill me. I had no ability to
cope with decisions that had to be made until I remembered I had
the mind of Christ (see 1 Corinthians 2:16). I got to the place where
I refused to cry because the tears released the suffocating pain of
my loss. He taught me to trust Him to turn suffering into glory. I
was learning what *blind faith* really meant. It meant I trusted Him
when I didn't understand why this was happening, or where the
Lord was taking me in this particular lesson. I simply trusted Him.

One really hard lesson was to trust Him to bring good out
of some evil harassment I was experiencing. I was fighting fear
and bewilderment, and kept asking for understanding. The activity
involved some neighbors behind me who were retaliating for the
harsh treatment my husband had used to get their dogs to stop barking all night. The neighbors worked all night, so of course the dogs

didn't bother them. Even after Bill died, they continued breaking things in my back patio; they put bizarre things under my bedroom window, and destroyed the watering system for hanging plants.

I prayed fervently for the Lord to move them out, to show me what to do, to bring them into Christian faith. You can see I had no idea what to do in my desperation. Winter was coming and the kids at church had a project selling WWJD bracelets to help missionaries. (What would Jesus do?) I said, "Okay, Lord, what *would* You do?" The answer seemed so simple. I bought half a cord of oak wood and racked my brain until I thought of one nice thing my neighbor had done. When I knew he was home, I went over and knocked on his door. I heard ferocious growling and barking, and he answered the door with one hand on the dog collar and one on the screen. I said, "I wanted you to know how much I appreciate all the work you did on our adjoining parkway. I have just had some wood delivered and you are welcome to use as much as you like."

As soon as I did what I thought Jesus would do, the harassment stopped. Not too long afterward, he moved away and the Lord brought me wonderful new neighbors. Sometimes the Lord uses other fingers to squeeze the grapes, rather than His own. My part is to submit to His will no matter who is doing the squeezing! Approaching my neighbor was a scary thing to do; he was not a nice man. The Lord assured me that He was my shield, my courage and most important, that this was what He would do!

What was the lesson I learned through all this? Fear is not from Him, and if I will obey what He is asking of me, He will do all the rest! All I have to do is trust Him.

I shall never forget being asked to speak to a group of widows. I sought the Lord for what He wanted me to share and He brought to my mind the different trials and troubles, with the scriptures I had been given that helped me through them. Years later, women who were at that little workshop have come to me telling what a blessing that meeting was, giving them hope to go on with their lives. I obeyed the Lord in fear and trembling and He took those feeble efforts and encouraged His daughters. Isn't that what we want to do? Turn our trials into triumphs so that He can use us for His glory and help others find their way.

Every victory of my life was all from Him; in myself, I would fail every time. The Apostle Paul tells us in that he considered the sufferings of this present time not worthy to be compared with the glory that is about to be revealed to us and for us, and conferred on us (see Romans 8:18)! How unspeakably marvelous it is to know Him.

Now when I feel the pressure, I know He is trying to separate the juice of the fruit of the Spirit from the waste in my life. Put another way, He is asking me to reckon my self-life dead unto sin and my spirit life alive unto God!

Each new day I wait for Him to reveal the plan He has for me and the path I am to take. In His love He comforts me, in His wisdom He guides me and in His strength He shield and protects me. He does all this for me; but the greatest joy of my life is when He chooses to use me and I become that poured out wine that He can use to help others.

God's Promises, God's Power
Our Choice

The Lord uses the Winepress to squeeze from us the self-life. He has a perfect plan and wants our trust in Him that He will take all our pain and turn it to good and use it for His glory.

Recognizing that God knows everything, we can conclude He knows exactly how to remove that in us that will hinder His plans.

❖ Will I submit to the pressure He brings in my life, *trusting Him* that His way truly is better than mine?

Tenaciously holding onto my rights and refusing to let go of dreams, goals and plans, that are no longer possible to obtain, is hard to do, but it is a choice I must make.

❖ Do I see His love in all the 'squeezing' as He whispers so softly, "My plans for you are better than the 'rights' you cling to."

Pruning is always necessary if the Master of the vineyard is to have a healthy crop of fruit.

❖ Asking Him to please tend my Vineyard (life) will I then *choose to obey and submit* to the painful pruning that is necessary for Him to accomplish His goal in me?

Chapter Three

Streams in the Desert

See, I am doing a new thing!
Now it springs up; do you not perceive it?
I am making a way in the desert and
streams in the wasteland.
Isaiah 43:19

Streams in The Desert

Barren wasteland, dry and parched
stretching before me endlessly,
in my thirst I cry to You.

You give me, not a pond or stream,
but an underground river,
rising up, flowing continueously.

This chapter deals with the times of refreshing that the Lord brings to us when we are dry, depressed and empty.

He meets us in our deep need with the very thing He knows will give us that encouragement we need to help keep us going.

We go through many emotions such as, bitterness, which the Lord wants to turn into sweetness. There are times when we are filled with anxiety, but our Lord wants us to receive His peace.

The amazing thing is He wants to give us all these benefits abundantly, not a pinch here or there, but overflowing and continuously.

These are His ways and times of refreshing in our journey through the wilderness.

Times of Refreshing

The Lord tells us in both the Old and the New Testament to forget the former things. In fact it is a command: "Forget the former things; do not dwell on the past…" (Isaiah 43:18, see also Philippians 3:14). He then goes on to tell us that He "…is making a way in the desert and gives us streams in the wasteland" (Isaiah 43:19).

All of us have different sets of circumstances when we lose our spouses, but we can know that God has hand-tailored each trial in our lives to fit His purposes. For me it was the care of my elderly mother. As an only child the responsibility was on my shoulders. My husband had been a tremendous help and he was no longer there by my side to help me. My Dad had died some years before so mother was also alone.

My mother was very demanding and as long as I didn't try to go on with my life but stayed right with her, all was well. I had been involved in my church in Bible study and intercessory prayer for years, and with the loss of Bill I needed those contacts more than ever. Each time I explained to my mother that I needed to get back to that part of my life (and invited her to go with me) she would become angry and demand to move back to her own condominium; so I would move her back. This happened three different times in a period of less than two years and left me exhausted each time. My guilt was terrible because I could only stay with my mother so many days without wanting some form of relief.

Living without my husband had become a terrible dry desert, and I certainly felt I was living in a wilderness. The devil found fertile ground to bury me in self-pity and guilt because of my longing for Bill and the constant caring and trying to please my mother. I had not only lost my husband but it seemed to me I had lost my life as well.

The Lord sent a lovely stream of refreshing water during this period by having my pastor's secretary call and say that my pastor wanted me to lead the prayer for women that Sunday night at a special Prayer Rally.

I went to the Lord and said, "Surely, Lord, that can't be You asking me to do this." The Lord let me know this invitation was indeed from Him as I prayed and asked Him to show me so I would not make a mistake.

The next morning while reading Oswald Chambers' *My Utmost for His Highest*, the Lord answered my prayer. I read,

> *"If when God said "Go," you stayed because you were so concerned about your people at home, you robbed them of the teaching and preaching of Jesus Christ Himself...as long as you would not obey, you were in the way..."*

I knew I would not be teaching or preaching, but praying. Nevertheless, I knew the Lord was telling me to "Go!" What a blessing for me to know that the Lord wanted to use me in this way even when I felt I was a total failure.

The time spent with my mother taught me many lessons, mainly about what the Lord wanted to do in me. But another lesson was the importance of praying for other caretakers. The care for my mother went on for three years. It was a hard time and a heart-breaking time, but oh, the lessons I learned! Like everything else in life the Lord teaches us, it isn't enjoyable while you are going through it, but you wouldn't take any thing for the valuable lessons learned once the trial is over.

Another splash of cool water the Lord sent during this time was a phone call from dear friends saying they were bringing a picnic over to share with us. That was such a fun time for all of us and especially for my mother and me.

During this time I was trying to finish the up-dating in my kitchen that Bill and I had begun before he died. Thank goodness, we had already bought three new appliances: stove, refrigerator and dishwasher. That was a culture shock as prices had gone up so much since our last purchases. The Lord knew I needed Bill for those huge decisions.

As mother moved in and out with me, progress in the kitchen would take place with getting the painting done, the new flooring installed or whatever else was needed during the times when she would be in her condominium.

Also during this time my air conditioning went out, which was a very big expense—and no Bill to talk it over with. And then as I started to catch my breath from that, my garage door fell off! My son was such a big help through all these trials. Either he would come fix it himself or he would know someone who could. During all these things the Lord was continually comforting me, giving me just the right word during my devotionals, or sending that perfect person with a love hug. I knew He truly would "…work all this together for good…" (see Romans 8:28).

Our Women's Bible Study was having a retreat and the Lord made it possible for me to attend by providing care for my mother. The theme that year in Bible study was being a servant. We were to write out what that meant to us and take it to the retreat. Here is what I wrote in my journal.

A true servant is one emptied of self. To verbalize a desire to be that true servant is giving God permission to place us in a crucible until all that is left is the river of Living Water flowing out to others. The pain, darkness, self-loathing, brokenness is all part of being formed into the image of Jesus. When our Father is finished then we are His servants.

To be a true servant – I must be filled with the TRUE SERVANT!

Thanks Lord, I needed to talk this over with You. I need to make a complete submission to Your will and I haven't done that yet, have I? There is a great sorrow in me Beloved, (this sorrow was more than my grief for Bill). Can You tell me why? I seemed to hear Him whisper, 'There is always great sorrow when we lay the longings of our heart in the grave. Remember the kernel of wheat.' I could only respond, Thank You, Beloved.

I was so blessed at the retreat. Years later, I am still learning how to get out of the way and let the True Servant live through me.

As my first year without Bill drew to a close I recorded thoughts of what I felt the Lord was trying to show me. He was teaching me a greater depth of faith than I had ever known; in fact, felt I had been on a crash course about faith. I knew I was getting to know my Lord as I could never have known Him otherwise. The big lesson was learning that God was in total control of every minute of every trial, and He was never surprised - I was!

On Bill's first year anniversary of being with the Lord I wrote,

"Oh, my Bill, how I miss you. This has been the most painful year of my life. But God! The Lord has given me more victories than I have ever had in my life."

The victories were those times He sent streams of water to encourage and refresh me, as I learned to live without my earthly husband, while getting to know the wonder of my heavenly Husband.

My final words in that first year journal were words of praise to my savior, Jesus.

"Thank You for being such a loving heavenly Husband. I know You are caring for me now. I know You shield me, protect me, guide me, bring just the right person at the right time to help with what ever problem needs "fixing." You have done all this for me because - Your Word promised that You would (Hebrews 13:5) . Thank You for giving me such a love for Your Word and for sending the blessed Holy Spirit to guide and enlighten me to what You are saying."

The important thing I was learning was to keep my eyes on Him and to expect Him to send streams of refreshing to me as I walked through the wasteland.

The Valley of Baca

The Valley of Baca (see Psalm 84:6) has been translated by many as the valley of weeping. Scofield's reference Bible calls it the valley of misery. For me it has been both. I thought of how we are told that God places all our tears in a bottle so only He is aware of how many of His children have gone through the valley of weeping (see Psalm 56:8). In one of my harder self-pity days I asked the Lord how He could possibly have room in His bottle for the tears of anyone else when mine alone would fill His bottle!

Things were so hectic during this period of my life that I felt stretched to the very end of myself. My mother was selling her condo and there was so much to do—packing, deciding what to keep and what to sell, at what price. I didn't have room in my home for all mother's things so I had to sort out what she would like to live with or give away or sell or put in storage. Her condo was in another city as well as her doctor. The need to drive back and forth from my house to hers went on for weeks and then months.

I wanted to run away and I asked the Lord if He couldn't use me on the mission field in some far-off land. I shall never forget His answer to me. "THIS IS YOUR MISSION FIELD!" Some days I came home so exhausted I just wanted to fall in bed and pull the covers up over my head. My heart ached for my precious mother as this was all hard on her too.

The one commitment I had not given up was our Wednesday Intercessory Prayer group. That next Wednesday when I went our leader took one look at me and said, "Dotty, we are going to intercede for you!"

Those friends knew the basics of what I was going through but they knew nothing of the daily trials, troubles and heartaches that were going on, only the Lord knew that. I felt like He was saying, "Okay, daughter, it's time to call for reinforcements!" I didn't resist. The girls started praying for me; the Holy Spirit gave each one of them a different zone of praying. I started crying and crying. The television show, *Life-styles of the Rich and Famous* ran across my mind. Mother and I had watched that show several times. I thought of the millions of dollars these people had spent on yachts, homes, etc. While my sisters were praying I thought this is the true wealth, having sisters who love you so much they can discern the needs and intercede in the power of the Holy Spirit. I felt enveloped and wrapped in God's love, care and provision. It was amazing just as He is amazing in meeting our needs when we don't even know what to ask for. And so He gave me refreshing while in the Valley of Baca.

This new life of learning to walk as a widow has been filled with tests and struggles and many tears. The paradox is even when I feel like a wimp I seem to feel myself growing stronger. Whether it is a trial, a temptation or a bout of weeping, the Lord comes alongside to strengthen and encourage me.

The Israelites passed through the Valley of Baca, but they didn't settle there. It was part of their journey. The valley of weeping is part of my journey also. When grief overwhelms me there is that temptation to sink down and dwell in Baca. Then I read in Psalm 107:35 that the Lord turned the desert into pools of water and parched ground into flowing springs.

How I thank You, Lord, for causing my parched soul to be refreshed by Your flowing springs! You are my example, Lord. You wept but it didn't keep You from doing Your Father's will. I marvel at how You carry me along in all my weakness, refreshing me at just the perfect time. You listen to my deep sighs and I can almost hear You say, "Come! The best is yet to be."

I thanked the Lord for holding my hand and giving me strength as I struggle to overcome each adversity, and for turning my Valley of Baca into pools of refreshing, streams of opportunities and rivers of blessings.

The God of Abundance

Wilderness places are a necessary part of anyone's journey through life. I had only to look at the Israelites who had turned an eleven-day journey into forty years because of their rebellion and unbelief, to know my choices would determine how long I would wander in the wilderness. I didn't want to stay in this dry, unbearable, lonely place forty years. I continually asked the Lord to show me what it was He wanted to do in me and what I was to learn.

The first thing He wanted to teach me was to be quiet. I had no idea how extremely hard that was to do. Then I understood why it was the wee small hours of the morning when I usually heard from Him—that was the only time I was entirely quiet!

The second lesson I felt He was teaching me was to wean myself away from the necessity of being with someone all the time. As a consequence of needing to learn these two lessons, I was in the wilderness once more.

As the days and weeks went by I realized my spiritual ear began to listen more intently for the checks of the Holy Spirit, for His guidance to do or not to do a certain thing. I was learning to relinquish control on my life and submit to the Lord's leading and control. The Lord knew my heart and He knew that I hadn't been in rebellion as I sought advice from others or attempted to walk in my own knowledge. He knew I was literally learning to walk alone on these new pathways of life. He was teaching me to find strength and direction from Him.

It was the strangest thing but I struggled to find balance in my walk. I never realized how much strength I gained from my husband. For example, it seemed I was forever locking myself out of the house or my car. When Bill was here that was never a problem as he would be there to let me in the house or have another key to the car. Through that I learned to have extra keys to everything in strategic places.

Another crazy thing I did was to be forever setting off my security alarm. It finally dawned on me to pray about that. Of course the Bible does tell us "…you do not have because you do not ask" (James 4:2 NKJV). I said, "Lord, You have to help me. Look what I'm doing all the time. You are my husband now, so help me stop this." And the amazing thing is that He did. Each time

I would reach for the door to open it, ever so softly I would hear "Alarm." The same thing would happen if I started to open a window before I had turned my alarm off.

Someone reading this who is not a widow will probably think, *what does locking yourself out of house and cars and setting off alarms have to do with learning to find balance in your walk again?* I'm not sure I can explain this behavior but to me half of myself was gone. I was listing to one side expecting my other half to hold me steady. That half was gone and I was in the process of learning to balance myself with what was left. My husband and I were one, we shared everything, our thoughts, plans, goals. We took care of each other in all these areas. Now there was no longer any one there to say, "Don't forget to turn off the alarm." "Do you have your extra car keys in your purse?" So I turned to my heavenly husband (see Isaiah 54:5) and said, "Lord, You are going to have to balance my lop-sidedness." He is always there but I had to learn to turn to Him and not to a husband who was no longer here.

I remember at one point telling the Lord that I couldn't tolerate the dry barrenness of my life anymore. He brought to my mind the extreme thirst the Israelites had in the wilderness. The Lord told Moses to strike the rock so that life-giving water would flow for them. (See Exodus 17:6)

I had read about a phenomenon that takes place in the desert where igneous and sedimentary rocks come together in the sides of the mountains. The extreme pressure of the occasional flashflood on the walls of the canyons sometimes hollowed out great fissures inside. These hollow mountains can become literal reservoirs holding thousands of gallons of water. Some Bedouin shepherds know of this and are able to take their heavy staff and when they strike the rock at the right place the blockage is loosed, allowing the water to gush forth.

I thought of how 1 Corinthians 10:4 speaks of the Lord as being my Rock. I knew, in the instant I remembered that scripture, how very much He wanted to bless me with the rivers of living water that He promised to every believer (see John 4:10–13). He was waiting patiently for my faith to see Him as that Rock of refreshing that would quench every thirst and bring verdant growth of faith in His ability to provide every need for me.

My heart filled with thankfulness for the teaching of this last experience. Learning to use the quietness of the wilderness enabled me to quiet my own spirit so I could hear my Lord speak to me in that "still small voice." The very quietness of this desert experience forced me to quicken my senses to become aware of His voice, His leading, His presence with me continually. These were lessons I would never have learned otherwise, because of the many voices and sounds that surround me in my everyday life.

The Lord was teaching me about priorities and how important it is to let Him set them. I had learned years before that when I didn't learn a lesson the first time, the Lord just put me back to take another lap around the mountain until the lesson was learned!

My faith was seeing more and more how He was a God of abundance. No matter how bleak, dry or barren my life might seem, I knew my Rock (Jesus) held overflowing blessings. If all my eyes could see was a sheer wall of rock (the impossible circumstances) I would remain sterile and dry. It was when I tapped my Rock (Jesus) with eyes of faith that I saw the God of the impossible do the impossible. He immersed me in an unlimited supply of living water which is wisdom, strength, faith, new directions—whatever my need might be. The Rock of Ages had all the answers for me. All that was needed to receive this tremendous abundance was faith in what He had promised. Then my desert would bloom in the glory of His abundance.

I have concluded that wilderness experiences are an essential part of God's plan if He is to complete His work in me. My part is not to resist where He is leading me, whether desert or oasis. My part is to learn the lesson that He has for me with each new journey. His abundance gives me hope in my times of despair, joy in my sorrow and He knows how to quench my every thirst with His Living water.

From Bitter to Sweet

Dealing with bitterness is a serious business. The Lord warns us not to let a root of bitterness spring up within us, thereby defiling many around us (see Hebrews 12:15). I have seen it happen that one person in her bitterness turned sisters and brothers against each other and that bitterness eventually even affected the cousins, leaving that particular family splintered.

Bitterness means "resentment, sourness". People who are bitter do have a sour look about them. They are also usually negative and complaining people, I certainly didn't want to end up being sour and full of resentment. However, there were times when I could identify with the Israelites and their journey in the wilderness. They had been marching three days without water as they traveled from the Red Sea to Marah. They were desperate for water but the well at Marah was bitter and they could not drink the water.

Sometimes in my journey through desert places I would become so dry that bitterness would try to creep in. I found that memories can be dangerous as they can be so poignant or pierce my heart. Other times the different circumstances I found myself in brought severe and harsh consequences so that I constantly fought that old devil question, "Why me?"

One of the most severe trials was the remembering that I wouldn't grow old along with my husband. I have already told that story in this book, but I had to continually fight for the victory to be *content* with that fact so that bitterness could not get a foothold on my heart. Another memory that hurt was remembering relationships that my husband and I had enjoyed that were no longer part of my social life. This caused me to experience the feeling of rejection from some persons who had been part of our lives. There was nothing I could say or do regarding this hurtful occurrence and in my silence I was again fighting bitterness.

What a wonderful Savior we have! Just as He brought the Israelites from Marah to Elim (which had plenty of water and even palm trees for shade), He brought me from my parched state to abiding under the shadow of His wings (see Psalm 57:1) that was my comfort and solace. As I abided (or rested) in Him I saw that the separating of certain relationships was necessary as God had a path I was to walk on and He planted me with others who were going in the same directions. He knew we would draw strength from one another. In my oasis of refreshing, He once again gave in abundance. For every person I missed being in my life, it seemed He brought so many more to take their place.

When bitterness wedges its way in, the Lord never lets me stay there. He quickly pricks me with conviction so I might confess and hurry on to the place of refreshing where the waters are sweet. More and more I see that it is my *choice*. Do I choose to be bitter or do I choose to trust my heavenly husband who sees the big picture of my life? Most of us know that His thoughts towards me are for good and not evil, to give me hope in my final outcome (see Jeremiah 29:11). The question is: Do I believe Him and His promises?

I was learning more and more that faith will always be the bottom line of what the Lord is trying to teach me. I always think of that short little sentence the Lord asked in the Gospel of Mark, "Will I find faith when I come?" That question pierces my heart and makes me feel like jumping up and down and saying, "Yes, Lord Jesus, yes! I promise to be full of faith when you come!"

Then the trials come and I am back to choosing whether to believe Him or not. All this has made me realize that I am making choices daily and how very important it is to make the right ones. When it is all said and done, why would I be so foolish as to choose the dry, parched desert of my own will, when I can have all the streams, rivers, and living water of His will?

The more I contemplate how very wonderful the Lord is, the more I want to sing the song Moses sang: "Who is like You, O Lord, among the gods? Who is like You, glorious in holiness, awesome in splendor, doing wonders?" (See Exodus 15:11) Amen? Amen!

Transforming The Desert
(And My Life)

There is a beautiful verse that I want to share with you, my readers. For all who are like me, a widow, these verses are for you. Let the beauty and wonder of these words sink into your soul. Take hold of the promises, knowing that He who promised is faithful and true and will perform what He has said.

> "...He will comfort all her waste places;
> He will make her wilderness like Eden,
> and her desert like the garden of the Lord;
> Joy and gladness will be found in it,
> thanksgiving and the voice of melody."
> Isaiah 51:3 (NKJV)

Oh what beautiful promises those are! How wonderful to know that He is aware of all my waste places, and certainly knows how dry the wilderness is. He can send rain and storms and create streams to flow in the desert. The parallel here is that He does the same thing in my life. The rain and storms (trials and tribulations) are used to help me see the great need for moisture (tears and suffering) to cause the verdant growth of faith that He is looking for in me.

At the time of this writing we had been in a drought condition for several years in California. That winter the Lord sent an abundance of rain. The desert soaked up every drop and was ready to show off when Spring came. I was more than ready for a change in my life so I grabbed an overnight bag and took off for the desert to see the flowers.

As I drove along the freeway absorbing the beauty flashing by, my mind kept dwelling on the many trips across this same desert my husband and I had taken. The pain of missing him was acute and there was a big hole in me where my other half used to be. My mind was dwelling on some of the promises the Lord had given me several months before. I knew I was to put my trust in Him and in the plans he had for me. The Lord had never told me not to grieve, but I knew it would please Him when I reached the point where I trusted Him not only for today, but for the future. I *wanted* to do that but I couldn't seem to dig myself out of the sandpit of doubt.

There were three steep grades on my journey that day, and at the summit of each one a carpet of beautiful flowers was spread out that was glorious. I could not control the laughter that bubbled up inside me at the sheer extravagance of it all. Driving with one hand and clicking my camera furiously with the other hand, I tried to capture the beauty of the panoramic scene, even though I knew my camera could never cover the scope of such a view. I seemed to hear the Lord whisper to me, "You cannot see the scope of the future life I have for you. Just as you have laughter now at the beauty I have created in this barren desert, so your new life will dispel the barrenness of the desert you are now walking in and you will rejoice in the beauty I have created for you."

My heart and mind grasped this wonderful message. "Oh, Lord, thank You, for creating all this grandeur so You could give me this message of hope." (I did know that this magnificent vista was for everyone, but you have to know I felt very exclusive at this point!) I shall never forget the enchanting riotous colors that danced and sparkled with each mile. The desert had once again offered itself up for all to see the glory that only the Lord could create.

Returning home I expected to walk in and have this new glorious life the Lord had promised materialize before me. Instead, the sky fell in with jolts, bumps and scrapes that were so painful. The Lord showed me a new thing about pain, that there are different kinds. In one week I experienced incredible, unspeakable and suffocating types of pain. These were the result of broken relationships, health problems, financial worries and deterioration of all kinds in the house and yard. I felt like I had walked into a nightmare. "Where is the beauty You promised me, Lord? And all that laughter, what happened to it?"

The most distressing pain was probably a broken relationship in my own family. The health problem was mine, gall bladder surgery. In the yard the sprinkling system had all gone either haywire or was broken. Nothing seemed to be working. The house had problems with carpeting, drapes and badly needed painting. I learned I had out-of-state company coming to visit, and I hadn't finished redoing the house.

Instead of peace, I was sleeping in split-shifts, if at all. I was confused, confounded and thinking how I could have been so wrong about what I *thought* I heard the Lord saying to me. Once more in the very early hours of the morning I heard that still, small voice whispering, "Trust Me." Pondering the grandeur I had seen in the desert and recalling what I thought were His promises to me, I wondered what the Lord wanted me to see and hear in all this. As I lay sleepless on my bed I asked those questions, light began to permeate through all the circumstances and I remembered that wildflowers fade, wilt and die. The green mountains turn brown in the summer and the desert becomes dry and barren once more. What is it that never changes? Jesus! His beauty is from everlasting to everlasting. My trials and tribulations are ordained by the Lord and do not matter; they are only opportunities of situations I can bring to the Lord. I knew His promises were true and unfailing. The Lord was after my faith again and either I will trust Him or turn aside. He will never violate my free will, it is always my choice. If I choose to trust Him Then He is free to transform my life.

I decided to offer up the sacrifice of praise and thanksgiving. That's what we do when we haven't seen anything of the fulfillment of the promise but we believe Him to perform what He said He would do. And as I chose to do that I *knew* He would make my wilderness an Eden and my desert a garden of the Lord. The jolts, bumps and scrapes in my life are like the new contours a flash flood brings to the desert. I have learned that the dry, barren places can become profuse with beauty when His touch is on the circumstances of my life. The Lord wanted to transform my life into His plan for me. What is His plan for me as well as for all of His children? He longs to conform us into the image of His Son.

This much I have learned: whether the Lord is causing a desert to bloom or transforming my life, He is always extravagant, profuse and lavish and I can always trust Him with my very life even in the painful transformation stage. Selah.

God's Promises, God's Power
Our Choice

Walking through desert places can be exhausting; sometimes it is hard to believe we will ever reach the end of this particular journey. I'm sure that is why the Lord places streams and rivers of refreshing in strategic areas of our lives, not wanting us to give up.

Walking through those times of bitterness, do we trust His nudges to turn our eyes on Jesus, *knowing* He can turn the bitter to sweet in our lives?

❖ Clinging to resentment and bitterness leads to a life of negatism. Is that where we want to live? Flinging off every negative thought and *clinging to His promises* for that abundant life is sunshine to the soul.

Living in the Valley of Baca (weeping or misery) is part of our journey as widows – but we do not have to stay there!

❖ When self-pity wraps itself around us, do we enjoy the deep misery that brings, or do we choose to crawl up out of the pit into the light and life He has for us?

When the Lord is digging those furrows and culverts in our lives, (through tests and trials), do we only see despair? It's possible to look up higher and see through His eyes the future rewards of glorious blossoms and fruit He is planting.

❖ Removing thorns and briars, which prohibits healthy growth, is painful. Do we resist and complain? The better way is to submit to the brief pain – allowing the Lord to perfect us so that He might shower us with His blessings.

Chapter Four

The Sunsets of Life

"You are never at any time nearer to God than when under tribulation, which He permits for the purification and beautifying of your soul."
Miguel De Molinos

The Sunsets of Life

"Your sun shall no more go down,... for the Lord shall be your everlasting light, and the days of your mourning shall be ended."
Isaiah 60:20 AB

Just as the sunset each evening signifies the close of the day, so are there sunsets in the widow's life when that which is past must come to an end.

This section deals with lying to rest some of our fears, our hopes and—perhaps the hardest part —the dreams and goals of the years ahead that we had planned to live with our husbands. It is a very comforting thought to me to know that our Lord knew before the foundation of the world how many years I would be a widow and so He planned a Chapter Two, so to speak, for the new life He has waiting for me. (Ephesians 2:10)

I hope it gives you comfort, too, to realize that the Lord eagerly waits for us to agree to the plans He has already made for our lives.

Only my heavenly husband has the wisdom to know the future and I have learned to trust Him with mine. Stamping closed on a way of life we had with our husbands is hard and painful, but it is necessary if we are to go on with the business of living the life the Lord has for us.

With the healing of time our sunsets become beautiful once more and we experience them with a sense of fulfillment and accomplishment as we begin that walk into our new life.

Learning to Trust for the Future

The scripture under the sunset picture gave me great encouragement – "…and the days of your mourning shall be ended." For me mourning was a paradox, part of me wanted it to be over and done with, but another part of me wouldn't let go.

One of the things I desperately needed to get behind me was the memory of our time together each day. Whatever our day had been, come twilight—that time not yet evening, and no longer day—was our time. We would sit and talk, discuss problems or dreams or goals. Didn't matter, we shared that time and made plans together.

In the beginning I would stand at my window and look at the sky and cry and cry and cry. It was horrible! That went on for a long time until finally I couldn't stand it any longer and began to make plans to be doing something that time of day. I like to cook and I like to read, so I would occupy myself with one of those things. Or, I would call a friend who was also single and visit with her until the sun had set. Learning how to struggle through that time of day wasn't easy, but keeping busy helped me think of something else besides how much I missed Bill.

I found that memories and routines that I had had with Bill were no longer a pattern of my life without him and even though painful, needed to be put to rest. One part of our routine that was very hard for me to give up was the trip to Baja, California in August that we had made for the past fifteen years. Living in Riverside, California, it was always wonderful to head for the ocean and leave all that heat behind us. Bill had died in August and as his first anniversary of being gone loomed ahead of me it was almost unbearable. I cried, prayed, and asked the Lord to remove all desire of even wanting to take off for Baja to be taken from me.

Did He do that? No. My life was changed and so patterns of my life had to change. Had the Lord babied me and made a way for me to go, it would have been just as hard the second year. However, in that second year I did go to Baja with my daughter for a week. It was terrible, not because of my daughter, but because of the jarring fact that Bill was not there and nothing was the same without him. After that experience I must have been weaned enough that the Lord was able to take that desire away and that battle was put to rest.

In August of 2004, Bill's 13th anniversary of being gone, my daughter and her husband asked me to go down with them. They turned our week down there into a nostalgic time of wonderful memories. We went to all the favorite eating places, shopping, etc. Places that Bill and I had loved and always enjoyed while we were there. The picture of the sunset at the beginning of this chapter was taken many, many years ago while Bill and I were having dinner at a restaurant right on the ocean. My kids took me there once more to enjoy all the beauty of the ocean and delicious food of that place.

Many years before that 13th anniversary, the month of August with all its yearnings and longings had been laid to rest. I pondered on why the Lord had given this wonderful gift to me through my daughter and her husband. I finally came to the conclusion it is part of His abundant life (see John 10:10) that He gives to us, and He gave me this magnificent gift to take the bad memories away from the last time I had gone down. Bill and I had fifteen years of wonderful memories in Baja and I believe the Lord wanted none of those to be dissipated, so He gave me a supremely fine ending to that chapter in my life. I find it hard to believe, but the Lord has given me a liking to be in Riverside during the month of August! I can hardly believe it myself! What a wonderful, amazing God we serve.

Another area where I was learning to trust Him for my future was in learning to wait for His guidance instead of running ahead of Him. Wanting to fill my time with worthwhile things, I would see a need and think, *Oh that is where the Lord wants me.* Inevitably I would meet with opposition of one kind or another. This happened to me several times and of course, I was wounded and confused, and I would cry out to the Lord asking why He wasn't doing something about all this. In His gentle love and kindness He directed me to the story of Isaac in Genesis 26:12–25. I had read this story many times before but had never really *seen* it.

The Lord blessed Isaac and he became very wealthy. He acquired large flocks of sheep and goats, great herds of cattle, and many servants. The Philistines became jealous of his wealth and filled up all the wells his father Abraham's servants had dug. Abimelech, ruler of the Philistines, asked Isaac to leave the country as he was too rich and powerful to remain among them.

Isaac's servants dug in Gerar Valley and found a gushing spring. The local shepherds came and said, "This is our water." They argued with Isaac's servants, so Isaac named the well *Argument*, and moved on.

They dug a second well and again there was a fight over it. Isaac named that well *Opposition*. Moving on, they dug yet another well, and the people finally left them alone. Isaac named this well *Room Enough*, for he said, "At last the Lord has made room for us, and we will be able to thrive" (see Genesis 26:22).

The Lord showed me in this story how profound Isaac's faith was. Isaac never argued, although his servants did. He knew this wasn't the place the Lord had for them. Meeting opposition at the second well, he still did not argue; trusting the Lord, he moved on. Finally, when the people no longer argued Isaac knew this was the place the Lord had for him and his people. There was *room enough*.

This story reminded me that all I had to do was trust the Lord to place me where He planned to use me. If I encountered arguments or opposition I was simply to move on until I too found that place where there was *room enough*. I wouldn't be ministering with Bill any longer and I knew the Lord was placing me in new and different areas. This was part of my new future and He was showing me how to recognize where He was calling me.

I found the principles I learned from Isaac's story were true whether for ministry or in relationships or different circumstances in my life.

As we face our sunsets we must be *willing* for the Lord to help us close these pages of our lives with our husbands. That part of our lives is over, the sun has indeed set upon them, but the Lord has a new day planned for us and we need to be willing to accept His plans. He is so gracious and loving that if we will do our part, He more than does His.

Watching the Sun Set on Planned Goals

Bill and I loved to travel and to experience God's lovely creation in different parts of the world. I shall never forget our first trip abroad. I longed to go to Israel and had all kinds of information ready for when the time came to hop aboard El Al, Israel's airline, and go see the land where Jesus walked!

In the middle of all my plans, my husband inserted his plans. We had gone out to dinner with friends and the husband of that twosome looked directly at Bill, not me, and said: "Bill, how would you like to go to Russia?" My heart churned; who would want to go to Russia? They were those wicked Communists (this was back in 1978)! They were known enemies of Israel.

Gathering all my thoughts together to let loose and expound on why we would never want to go to Russia, I heard my husband say with excitement in his voice, "Hey, I could really get into that!" He turned to me with a big smile on his face and said, "Honey, wouldn't that be a great trip?"

Being the wonderful Christian wife that I was, I smiled and said, "Well honey, it certainly something we can pray about." With that he and our friend were off and running with all the plans, such as time, airline, etc. Need I say our first trip abroad was to Russia? I can never thank God enough for that trip; it was there that I saw the world heart of God (see John 3:16). I fell in love with the Russian people and pray for them to this day.

Bill and I made many trips after that, and yes, we did make it to Israel. I loved all of them and especially the people. It always amazed me how language was never a barrier; we would learn a few words of that country and then use body language. We still had trips planned for the future when Bill died. I was born loving to travel so this was a hard chapter of my life to let the sun set on. In the following years I made several trips with friends but it was never the same without Bill.

The most beneficial trip I took after Bill died was with my daughter to Paris, France. A dear friend called from Northern California and said, "Hey, Dotty, do you want to go to Paris?" The Lord seemed to be saying, "Yes", so I asked my daughter if she would like to go with me and she seemed to hear a "Yes," also. There were sixteen of us on that trip, all women. We spent seven days in Paris and went out touring day and night. Monet is my favorite artist so I spent part of two days at the Orangerie admiring his famous painting "Lilies." Two full rooms were given over to viewing this incredible set of paintings; one in the round with four panels, overhead lighting, the other, oval with four panels and overhead lighting. I had no idea the original was so enormous. These rooms had to be 40 to 50 feet long with large oval sofas in the middle of the room where you sat and just looked. All this time I had thought Monet's "Lilies" were those few lilies on a pond that we see on post cards!

A very large park runs behind the Orangerie to the Louvre. There isn't any way to describe the Louvre. I was filled with awe as I gazed upon the Mona Lisa, Winged Victory, Venus de Milo and so much more. I kept saying, "Lord, look at this, it's the original, not a copy, not a print, but the *original*!" as though He wasn't there when the original was conceived and finished. I felt supremely blessed to have experienced even a small part of what the Louvre offered.

We made the trip in November 1992; one year and three months after Bill had died. It was the best thing I could have done. Why? For one thing it disrupted my routine, took me to new sights, let me see once more how large the world really is. I got all kinds of insights from the other women on the trip, I heard about their problems. However, none of us spent time dwelling on the negatives of life. When we returned home I had a new perspective for my life that was very much needed.

Just before we left I had submitted a poem to a publisher and they had accepted it for publication. The Lord used that to encourage me to get back into writing again. Before then, all the writing I had done was keeping a journal. (I highly recommend keeping a journal to everyone.) The trip was beneficial in many ways but the most important is what I have already mentioned, it gave me a new perspective which I desperately needed. All the trips we had planned that would never be were being laid to rest. This was very hard for me especially when I would hear from someone who had made a trip we had planned and I knew I would never make with Bill.

If you aren't one who likes to travel, do whatever it is that is special to you. Make yourself get out of your comfort zone. We can lose ourselves in nothingness and after awhile it doesn't seem to matter whether we move on or not. But it matters to God, and He has that wonderful new life for us that He wants us to enter into. We are all different and to some this might sound like a frivolous kind of thing to be laboring over so as to put it to rest. For me it was giving up that part of my life that Bill and I had so enjoyed having together, and I knew it had ended.

Around the world we have fellow sisters who are widows. Some because they live in a war-torn country, others because of dreadful diseases, and others whose husbands have died of accidental or natural causes. Whatever the reason we are widows, whatever the circumstances, God is faithful to every daughter.

His promises are true for those whose families are destroyed and their country ravaged. They look around them and see no husband, no home, and no electricity, even their water is hard to obtain. Food is scarce and they have a government with no money, struggling to implement even the simplest programs.

Is God unaware of the despair His daughters are experiencing? Absolutely not! I think of the story of Hagar in the book of Genesis. She and her son were in the desert with no water, no food and Hagar was sure they would die. She separated herself from her son because she couldn't stand to hear him cry as he was dying. The Lord heard him and saw her sorrow, and said, "What troubles you, Hagar? Fear not, for God has heard the voice of the youth where he is. Arise, raise up the youth and support him with your hand…" (see Genesis 21:17–18 AMP). Hagar obeyed the Lord and as she did, her eyes were opened and she saw a well and was able to get water.

The Lord had plans and a life for Hagar and her son just as He has a life and a plan for you, wherever you are, whatever your circumstances. He longs for us to believe His promises. Do we believe that He has already prepared paths ahead of time for us to walk on (see Ephesians 2:10)? He tells us to fear not, and not be discouraged, for He is with us (see Isaiah 41:10). Our bank is the Word of God, filled with promises which He longs for us to start cashing, so that He can bless us abundantly, lavishly.

There are widows all over the world; all in different situations, different circumstances; but the God we serve is no respecter of persons. He is the same yesterday, today and forever! He never changes, His promises are from everlasting to everlasting, His faithfulness endures forever and He loves us with an unfailing love! To *know* Him is to know He loves that widow in Liberia, in Israel, France, England, Sudan, wherever she might be, with the same caring, everlasting love. What each of us as widows must do is *believe* that He will do what He has promised.

Back to my world and the faithfulness of the Lord as He began to show me new kinds of trips; trips where I could take my camera and revel in the beauty of His creation. And wonder of wonders, with great joy I have learned that He is planning a missionary trip for me to minister to and encourage other widows. What a privilege that will be.

Just recently I borrowed my son's laptop and took off for a favorite spot for six days. There is a saying, "I'm comfortable in my own skin," and that is a gift the Lord has given me. I also love friends and family, so two of those days included being with them. The big bonus for me during this time was getting a whole chapter written for this book while enjoying the serenity and beauty of where I was staying.

Each time I have let the sun set on the big hurdles of my life that can be no more; I have been overwhelmed at what the Lord had planned all along to fill that place. He who causes the sun to rise each morning and set each night is not unmindful of the things in my life that He is asking me to let the sun set on. He has that new day already planned with all the splendor and majesty He alone can bring into our lives.

I know with each sunset of a dream, a goal, plans for the future that Bill and I had made, the Lord is saying, "Don't be afraid, for I am with you. Do not be dismayed, for I am your God. I will strengthen you. I will help you. I will uphold you with My victorious right hand" (Isaiah 41:10 NLT).

In light of all those wonderful promises, how could we not trust Him for all the sunsets that are needed in our lives? Whatever is in our future will be glorious because He will be there.

God's Promises, God's Power
Our Choice

Sunsets bring forth many emotions depending on where we are in our lives. We can see beauty, or pathos; for widows it is so important for us to remember, as we close the door on all that can be no more, God already has the new day planned for us.

❖ Are we holding tightly to what we have had, or, lifting open hands for Him to sift the past from the future – holding loosely whatever He gives us, because *we trust Him*.

❖ Looking into future years without our spouse beside us, is extremely difficult. Will we ask for *eyes of faith* to see that with every sunset of our dreams, plans, and goals, He holds sunrises full of hope?

Chapter Five

Walking Through Meadows

I have always thought of meadows as something lovely to stroll through. I am learning that I can hide in meadows, struggling with indolence, instead of climbing the heights and fighting regrets so as to make noble decisions.

Walking Through Meadows

*"God may not give an easy journey to the Promised Land,
but He will give us a safe one." - Bonar*

When I walk through a meadow I like to meander. That's such an old fashioned word, isn't it? However, at the meadow-stage of widowhood, it's a good word. We are beginning to see the light at the end of the tunnel but we are not quite there. We roam around with decisions that need to be made and we're still trying to put our memories in a right perspective—meaning that we try to enjoy them without the pain.

A lot of the time we are still dealing with regrets. Loneliness is a big issue with many widows. In my meadow I fought indolence. I couldn't seem to get motivated to do the things that so badly needed doing. Cleaning out closets and drawers is still a big difficulty for me.

Just as sunsets are a time to put some things behind us, I looked at my meadows as sort of a half-way house. The light had gone on in some areas of my life but I still lacked discipline and motivation.

As I sought the Lord about all this He brought to my mind these words:

We do not want you to become lazy, but to imitate those who through faith and patience inherit what has been promised. (Hebrews 6:12)

That was how I was to pray – for faith and patience. And that was the way I made it to the other side of my meadow.

Meadow of Indolence

Indolence is habit-forming, and it does breed laziness. At first I rather enjoyed walking through this meadow of indolence. I would do what was absolutely necessary and then get a book and lose myself in someone else's story. Being a voracious reader, I soon realized the library would be much less expensive than my local bookstore. The bag of books I brought home from the library was the maximum weight I could carry.

The more I read, the less motivated I felt to do housework or keep up with the weeds in my yard. I was totally unmotivated to do anything but read (I know this is also called escapism, or denial).

While doing my devotional one morning something I read made me think of the stories the Lord had given me about the three storms I had gone through while driving to see friends in Arizona not long after Bill died. The first storm had been a torrential rain. I could only see the two little red tail lights of the car ahead of me. The second storm had been a white-out of fog, and the third storm had been a fierce wind. After the journey I asked the Lord to explain to me why He felt I needed to go through these storms.

I felt He was telling me of the future storms in my life. The first storm was the fiercest and would last the longest. I felt this referred to the tremendous spiritual warfare that would come against me in accepting Bill's death. The second was fog which is an element of weather I dislike more than any other to drive in. Even though I could not see, yet I felt safe, I had no fear. The lesson of fog seemed to be, not to worry if my future seemed fuzzy or obscure. I was to plow through in faith, believing the Lord would take care of all the tomorrows and trusting Him to bring me into clear visibility right on His time schedule. The wind storm impressed me as an illusion, a tactic of the enemy trying to blow me off course. Again, I was to trust the Lord for wisdom and guidance. Between storms the Lord gave me sunshine, smooth driving and a time to seek Him in quietness.

It will soon be fifteen years of going through storms. The longest and most intense was becoming reconciled to my status as a widow. I wanted a blueprint for this new chapter in my life, but the Lord had said, "Accept the storms and trust Me."

When I was in phases where everything looked obscure and fuzzy, I reminded Him that He promised to hold my hand (see Isaiah 41:1 NKJV) and never leave me (see Hebrews 13:5 NKJV).

The wind storm was the enemy again, trying to sweep me off course. This storm would be the shortest storm of the three.

Back to my obsessive reading, I thought of the wind storm and how the Lord had warned me the enemy would try to embroil me in detours that would blow me off the path of life He had planned. I thanked Him for the wake-up call and asked Him to help me examine my reasons for enjoying the meadow of indolence. I seemed to hear, *Try the dictionary*. I did and there was my answer. I learned that indolence causes very little or no pain. I liked this back-path going nowhere because there was no pain as I meandered in and out of the lovely paths I found there.

I was back to learning more about faith and knew it was time for another growth spurt in my spiritual life. I wanted to inherit the promises in the Bible, and knew as long as I continued strolling through the meadow of indolence my spirit life would be stunted, stalemated and stagnant! So I asked the Lord to please set my priorities and then put iron in my soul so I would hear and obey. By this time I didn't trust myself in the least! I could almost hear the Lord give a sigh of, *Thank goodness*, as I was beginning to understand what He was trying to teach me. I was to trust in Him, not in myself! Hadn't I heard that before?

To this day I marvel at His patience with me but I'm so grateful that He doesn't give up on His children. Now when indolence beckons, and it does, I ask Him for a jump-start into whatever He has planned for me that day. No matter if I think He is aiming a little too high for me to obtain that goal, I *know* He will supply me with the power and motivation and see me through to the finish.

What have I learned? Walking through the Valley of Indolence is dead, dull and dreary. I most definitely have a choice that has to be made each day between apathy and interest in His plan for me. I much prefer climbing the heights with Him, and when we reach the summit He always takes my breath away with the abundance of beauty He longs to share with all His children.

Meadow of Decisions

To stay in my house or move?
Repave the driveway?
Who to buy a new air conditioner from?
Repair the roof or replace with a new one?

These were just a few of the decisions that I needed to make and Bill was not there to talk them over with. I intensely missed leaning on him for solutions and decisions.

That first year I thought if I moved it would be less painful than living in our home where Bill had made an impact of one kind or another in every room. Everywhere I looked I saw where he had changed this or hung that picture or mirror, painted, repaired, whatever. I even went so far as to find a condominium I knew would be perfect for me. But all the time I was praying, "Lord, please don't let me get out of Your will."

This went on for quite a few months until one Sunday I came home from church, by myself, to an empty home. Do you sense a bit of self-pity here? I sat on a chair in the corner of my living room and as I was sinking further into that black hole (again!), I looked up at the beams in my living room and heard as clear as a bell, *"You will miss him just as much if you move."*

Wow! I saw that condominium with all those bare walls, all those naked windows, all those empty rooms where furniture would have to tried first this way and then another. I said, "O my God, I understand, there would be no Bill to hang picture, mirrors, help me move furniture, do all those potted plants on the patio." At that point I knew I would miss Bill far more if I moved. I was fortunate that I loved our home and its location, so I didn't want to move for any reason other than trying not to miss my Bill too much. I thanked God profusely for being so *good* to me and helping me realize what a terrible mistake it would have been to move.

This does not mean that moving wouldn't be the perfect solution for other widows. We are all different, and our needs are different. I can't speak for anyone else, but I am prone to make mistakes and my Lord knows this so He has to keep a firm hand on me to keep me from plunging ahead to dangerous waters. The point here is to be sure it is what the Lord has for us.

Another decision had to be made about my cement driveway; it dipped just enough so that when we had a rainstorm the water emptied itself into my garage instead of flowing the other way into the street. I had no idea who to call or how to go about getting this taken care of. Bill took care of all that and somehow or other the garage was always empty of water while he was here. Not me, I had a mess and was running out of bricks to set everything on that was on the floor of the garage.

Once again I turned to my son (He has helped me with a multitude of needs all these years. Bill would be so proud of him). He knew just the person to call for the driveway but he also knew the back entrance to my house always became flooded when it rained. So he took it upon himself to send his men over (he is an electrical contractor) and dig a hole, lay an underground pipe, from my back steps to the street. Now when it rains my back entrance stays dry, my garage stays dry, and I thank the Lord for always giving me the abundance when He answers my prayers for decisions that have to be made.

My air conditioner went out that first summer Bill was gone. I called my son to tell him my latest woe. He gave me the name of a very reliable man to deal with and also advised me to buy a larger capacity air conditioner. He said, "Mom, you will use less electricity and save money." That sounded good to me, and he was right. So once again, in my meadow of decision, the Lord turned that problem to my benefit.

Every winter during the rainy season my roof sprang new leaks. I would run around placing my pots and pans in strategic places. It was a tile roof with the original hand-formed tiles. I felt to replace it would eat up my chidren's inheritance so I kept having it repaired. This time I called one of my pastors to see if he could recommend someone to do roof repair. He did and I used that company for several years. However, there came a time when I knew I had to replace the roof. My house was 72 years old and it still had the original roof!

I was so proud of myself when decision time came. I had been on my own almost twelve years and, with the Lord's wisdom, had begun to try making decisions by listening to His guidance. I called three well-known roof companies in town, prayed over their bids with the Lord, and with perfect peace made my decision. I got a new roof that I am delighted with, and I jumped up and down and clicked my heels together as I hadn't called my son, or my pastor, just called on the Lord.

This might sound silly to many people, but I doubt it does to widows. We are used to our husbands making decisions that involve any repair that is needed for our homes. We talk it over with them, yes, but as a rule husbands are far more knowledgeable and we rely on them.

What a tremendous sense of accomplishment to be able to make decisions without involving other people. I have always hated to be a burden to my children and most widows I know feel the same way. We don't like bothering them as they are all busy with their own lives. So, it is a double blessing when we have a problem, face it and solve it on our own.

I wish to make it very clear that I am never on my own. The Lord so directs, helps and shares His wisdom with me that I *know* He answers the cry of my heart when I say, "Please don't let me make a mistake." As with all new things that we must learn, we start with baby steps and progress until we feel we are able to start running in all these new areas of our lives. In the myriad decisions that must be made He is always there, sharing His wisdom,

93

directing our steps, helping us over the bumps and pitfalls, until we clearly see the way we are to go. Our heavenly Husband is so very careful with us as we walk in the Meadow of Decisions.

Meadow of Regrets

Wallowing in self-pity, steeped in regrets, I allowed the devil to bury me ten feet deep. He berated me with what a terrible mother I had been, for good measure he threw in terrible daughter. In this section, I will deal of how he convinced me I failed Bill. I felt I had done nothing right in my whole life. How could the Lord possibly love someone like me? I was bursting with regrets and buried under condemnation.

My sleep patterns were miserable. I hated myself and knew everyone else did also. Why had the Lord taken my husband and left me in this woeful condition? After all, my husband was the only one who had understood me and gave me unconditional love. I remember the more accusations the devil heaped on me the more I willingly received them. Lethargy curled around me like fog curls around trees as I walked in the meadow of regrets.

Only the Lord knows how long this period lasted, I didn't have the energy to keep a journal. I do know that when I reached the end of the pathway the Lord began to show me the form my grief had taken. In every aspect of my life the strength I had received from my husband was gone, I had not learned to yoke up with the Lord and draw from His mighty power. In my weakened condition the enemy was tossing me about like a dog playing with a bone.

As I turned to reading my Bible again, the Lord began to build my faith in amazing ways. He brought tests and trials that had no answers, and only through Him were the victories won. One of these amazing times was when I lost my wallet. While shopping I had taken it out to get some information and left it lying on the counter. I went ahead with my shopping and heard the intercom announce my name asking me to come to the head cashier. I did, and after they had verified who I was, she handed me my wallet. I didn't even know I had lost it! No money was taken, nothing in it was disturbed—I knew the Lord had done that for me. In thankfulness to the Lord, I left some money for whoever it was that had found it and turned it in.

The biggest lesson I learned was that regrets are not from the Lord. The enemy uses them to keep me looking to the past and especially past mistakes. The Lord deals with any mistakes I might make on a current level through conviction, repentance, confession and forgiveness, and always with great love.

Probably one of the most agonizing regrets for widows is the thought, *If I had done this or if I had done that, would it have ended differently?* The devil loves to beat us up with this thought of What if?

My husband and I were in Mexico when he became ill. On the long drive home that night we passed different places where I could have stopped and gotten help for Bill. He would not let me stop, he just kept saying, "I want to go home, Dotty." I believe now he knew how serious his condition was and he wanted to get *me* home.

He was giving a little grunt of pain with every breath. I was praying my head off out loud and silently, asking God to intervene, to help Bill, to heal him, finally I said, "Bill, do you dig pain so much you won't let me stop?" Again he said, "Dotty, I want to get home." Believe me, if I had known he was going to die nothing would have stopped me from rushing to the closest hospital. I had no idea he was so ill. But the doctor told me after Bill was gone that it wouldn't have made any difference even if I had gotten him to a hospital.

It was after all the tumultuous things were over that have to be done and taken care of for a funeral and the time came for me to begin living alone, then it was that the enemy, that old devil, started in. Always at night, usually late at night: *"If you had stopped in Chula Vista at the hospital there he wouldn't have died... If you had made him stop in Escondido he would still be alive…"* And on and on the litany went from that persistent enemy.

I wasn't sleeping. My regret had turned to guilt and finally to self-condemnation. I asked the Lord to help me, but I couldn't hear Him because I was never still long enough. This went on for several months until finally in the wee hours one morning I heard His voice saying "Are your times in My hands or yours?" (see Psalm 31:15a)

With that so many scriptures flew through my mind. "…You have determined their appointed times…" (see Acts 17:26). "There is an appointed time for everything, a time to give birth and a time to die…" (see Ecclesiastes 3:1–2) "And which of you by being anxious can add a single cubit to his life's span?" (see Matthew 6:27) There was another one, "You have decided the length of our lives. You know how many months we will live, and we are not given a minute longer." (Job14:5 NLT)

God hadn't abdicated, He was still on the throne; He was and is ever in total control! Hallelujah! I knew Bill died right on God's time plan, certainly not mine, and I knew also that the Lord has never made a mistake. It was His time to call Bill home.

With that I rolled over and went to sleep. The next time the devil started his false allegations of how I should have stopped and gotten care for Bill, I just started quoting all those scriptures out loud. He tried two or three more times and I answered each time in the same way, and finally he accepted defeat and stopped.

There are many different kinds of regrets, too numerous to try to cover most of them. Probably one of the most painful and poignant regrets is not being as good a wife as I knew I could have been. We may not admit that even to ourselves, but I know many of us wish we might have even the last year to live over to be just that wife men dream about.

Bill and I had a wonderful marriage, we enjoyed each other immensely and he would tell anyone that he had no complaints. In my heart I knew I could have made him feel like more of a king in his realm. I could have built him up so high that he would have felt he was sitting on the pinnacles of the mountain. He had so many marvelous talents I could have made him feel as wise as Solomon, the wisest man who ever lived.

If I had that year to live over again, would I do all those things? I would like to think I would. What kept me from doing it while Bill was here? I have given that a lot of thought. I suppose at the time I felt I was doing all those things. I boasted of his many abilities and praised him for being such a good husband and father. I thanked him many times for being such a tireless provider; we were a single-income family at his insistence. I went out twice and found good jobs after the kids were in school full time, but Bill would have none of that. He was the provider of his home, and he was a good one.

Looking back I know I could have raised the bar and built his esteem a little higher. A woman can value her husband in many ways. Her words are one way, and I believe he knew how highly I admired him and how much I loved him. Both of us always spoke of our love for one another several times each day. I was thinking more of the unspoken ways we express our admiration and love. By attitudes, those special looks, the deferring to him, especially among friends. I think I could have done more of that and wish I had.

Walking through the meadow of regrets has caused me to stop and contemplate on the ways I could have done things in a better way. The Lord has also taught me to use discernment on where that regret is coming from and how to use the spiritual tools He has given me to fight them.

Discerning when it is the enemy who is dragging me down into doubt, discouragement, fear or despair, I know from the beginning I am a winner because I stand in the victory Jesus has already won for me. I have learned in a new way how to enter into spiritual warfare. When I am speaking at a retreat, seminar or workshop, this has helped me to encourage the younger wives to be that wife the Lord has called and will equip her to be.

As I said in the Cover Page of this section, it is with faith and patience I walked through my meadow. It took patience to wait on the Lord for Him to show me which way to go, and faith to *believe* He will get me to the other side. Now I can stroll through my meadow with no regrets. I am free to enjoy the sweet fragrance of the Lord and His fellowship.

Meadow of Joy

Nehemiah is one of my favorite books of the Bible. His goal was to rebuild the wall around the city that had been destroyed and he used the rubbish, as well as new material, to complete his task. There is a Scripture passage in that book that blesses and encourages me greatly. "…and be not grieved and depressed, for the joy of the Lord is your strength and stronghold." (Nehemiah 8:10b AMP)

The Lord's joy is my strength. When my husband died my joy died with him. Through all the months of struggles and sorrows I learned more and more about Jesus. It was His word (the Bible) that comforted me; His promises that held and strengthened me.

The walls of my life were certainly down and rubbish was lying everywhere—the rubbish of dismay, depression and bewilderment of what to do with my life. I asked the Lord to help me rebuild and He did. When the rubbish began to overwhelm me I was amazed at how, unexpectedly, there would be someone calling or coming to my home that needed to be loved, prayed for, or encouraged to hope again.

After they hung up or left my home, I always felt so much better and I knew another hole in my wall had been rebuilt. The Lord did this repeatedly with all my rubbish until my wall was re-established. After each encounter I discovered more of His joy filling me. I was learning that my healing was being accomplished each time I reached out to help someone else. These encounters caused me to see and hear others' problems and concentrate on helping them, instead of being mired in the misery of my own.

I thought of the Israelites and their journey through the wilderness. I was identifying with them in my own wilderness experience. At one time they had a desperate need for water and the Lord gave them water. I remember the manna that never failed them for forty years. I contemplated the enemies the Lord defeated for them.

I reviewed in my mind the Lord's goodness towards me instead of pounding me over the head with all the rubbish in my life, like fear which chases faith away, indolence, reading His promises but not claiming them, and so much else cluttering up His will for my life. God took all that rubbish and turned it to good to rebuild my wall of faith. I realized the *joy of the Lord* was a result of heartfelt thankfulness for all He had done; how unspeakably wonderful to serve a God like that.

As I walk through this meadow of joy I lift up my heart to Him in praise, I bless Him with my whole heart. I thank Him that He is a God who cares when His people are grieved and depressed. I thank Him over and over that because of all He has done I rejoice in Him and His joy becomes my strength.

God's Promises, God's Power Our Choice

We each will have a meadow to walk through; how long it takes us to get to the other side is up to us. Most of us experience denial, regrets, and the big battle of facing decision-making without the comfort and strength of our husbands.

❖ When walking through that path of denial, are we willing to let the Lord help us to make the transition from the past to the future?

❖ Facing regrets and dealing with them can be a cloud over our heads for years. We need to ask the Lord for discernment in this area. If it is the devil stealing our peace from us, learn to refuse his lies, in the name of Jesus. If it is the Lord convicting us, take it to the Cross at once, confess whatever necessary, and *believe He forgives us and go on with our lives.*

❖ The key to victory here is to know we are not alone; the God of all wisdom is with us always. Will we stop, acknowledge Him and ask for His wisdom in dealing with whatever the problem is? He is always willing; our part is to stop, listen for His still small voice and to *trust Him?*

Chapter Six

He Gives Me Hinds' Feet

"Perseverance: a lowly virtue whereby
mediocrity achieves an inglorious success.
—Ambrose Bierce

He Gives Me Hinds' Feet

*"The Lord God is my strength, my personal bravery and
my invincible army; He makes my feet like hind's feet,
and will make me to walk (not to stand still in terror,
but to walk) and make spiritual progress upon my
high places (of trouble, suffering or responsibility)!"
Habakkuk 3:19*

Habakkuk 3:19 is one of my all-time favorite verses. When I first read this verse I knew I had to learn what a hind is! A hind is a small female deer. A little hind can mount upon the high places; sure-footed, she can balance on a rock. It is incredible to watch them scamper over sheer rock, absolutely fearless.

The Lord reminded me of this verse when Bill died. It was as if He was saying to me, You will have trouble, suffering and responsibility, but if you will put your trust in Me, I will do all I have promised and give you hind's feet that will enable you to walk and make spiritual progress.

The Lord was teaching me He is my Rock and as long as I am standing sure-footed on Him, He will never falter or fail me.

I also learned at that time that trouble, suffering and responsibility are very much a part of the Christian life. My part was to stand firmly on Jesus, my Rock; I could then trust Him to bring His glory and my good out of every trial.

I want to share some of the blessings we have because He gives us hinds' feet to climb and surmount every trial we encounter.

Hinds' Feet are for Climbing

The Lord had called me into ministry in our women's Bible study many years before Bill died. I was also involved in the women's intercessory prayer group at our church. Bill loved the men's Bible study and was always inviting his friends to come join with him.

With the exception of two family crises, I stayed connected to these two groups. The first time was with my mother, which I have already written about. The second crisis involved my two-year-old great granddaughter who was diagnosed with leukemia. I stepped down from ministry for a year to be with the family to help in any way I could. This was certainly one of those times of trouble spoken of in Habakkuk 3:19. The Lord gave us a wonderful promise in John 11:4 which we held on to like glue and *believed* what He promised. Erin is five now and pronounced leukemia free! Praise to the Lord for this bountiful blessing.

During these intervening years I was asked to speak, usually on prayer or on *fear not* in the Bible. I had written little booklets on each of these subjects. Each time I was asked to share I would earnestly seek the Lord for His will and whether it was really of Him. If He confirmed the call, I would accept. My mouth was dry, my heart was pounding, but each time the Lord faithfully saw me through. I was learning to take baby steps with my hinds' feet.

I remember one time at our church I was asked to do the teaching segment for our morning women's Bible study. I spent hours studying and praying about the lesson in Revelation chapter three. That was years ago and even now I could probably teach most of that lesson without notes. Also, we had a time limit. I am a firm believer in keeping on time, so I took my kitchen timer with me to the podium. Two of my friends sat in the back of the church and said they could hear that timer ticking away. I was petrified to get up there and teach these women and I knew I would not stay on time if I didn't have something right there in front of me. The Lord knew my fear and gave me hinds' feet to be able to complete my commitment.

In my eighth year of widowhood, 1999, the Lord began to move me into doing retreats for women in different churches. He has given me a great love for women, especially today. I feel they are bombarded by *everything* that opposes the Bible. They need to know that the Lord is well able to help them overcome any and all trials and temptations they might encounter. There were just a few retreats in 1999 as the Lord was taking me down a new path. I knew I had to build faith in Him in a new way. You hear a lot of voices when asked to do a retreat but it was essential to me that I hear just one—His.

In 2000 I was asked to speak at seven retreats. Each one was so unique and wonderful, and I always went with my heart pounding and clinging to the Lord; for His message, for His strength and His plan for these women. I fervently reminded Him that I needed those hinds' feet to accomplish what He was asking me to do.

I want to share about one that will always have a very special place in my heart. (They were all special, but this was a very small church and the women extraordinary in their hunger for the Lord.) They had chosen a mountain resort for their retreat and it was winter, so there was snow. I do not drive in snow, nor was I equipped with chains, tires, whatever you need. The weather man predicted clear skies, no snow. I said, "O God, thank You!"

As I turned off the freeway to begin my climb up the mountain I was singing along with my praise tape and enjoying the beauty all around me. There was snow along the sides of the two-lane highway and the greater the elevation the greater the snow banks. The tree branches were heavy with snow which made me think they looked like the Lord had covered them in ermine, it was a beautiful sight. At about 3500 ft. it began to snow. I began crying out to the Lord reminding Him that it was supposed to be clear; did He remember *I did not drive in snow*? At 4500 ft. altitude I was in a white-out and the snow was so thick my windshield wipers were having a hard time shoveling off the snow. God sent a pick up truck from somewhere and put it in front of me. All I could see was his big red tail-lights. My fingers were gripped so tight around my steering wheel that they were white all over, not just the knuckles.

You have never heard such fervent, earnest prayer entreaties! I said, "Lord, You could just send a little puff of wind and raise this cloud up, just enough to see Lord, okay, Lord? Okay, please Lord?" My hinds' feet (tires) were still clinging to the highway (a highway that I could not see) and then I lost the big red tail-lights. I don't know if he turned off or I just couldn't keep up with him. I said, "Lord, please don't give me a test now. I know you called me to do this retreat, I know You will get me there safely, but *please Lord* could You just give that little puff and raise the cloud?"

He did it! All of a sudden I could see all the cars in front of me; I could see the highway (the two-lane road, that is). I was filled and flooded with such joy I could hardly stay in the car. I wanted to roll my window down and shout to all those drivers, "Look what God did!" just so they would know it was God Who had done that for us, but I couldn't get my fingers off the steering wheel, they just would not uncurl. So I settled with filling my car up with praises.

The next trouble was in not being able to find the women. At the conference site there were little bungalows and big two-story bungalows, all with different names. I had no idea where my girls were. I drove all over and finally found a young boy and told him which house I was looking for. He didn't know either. I kept driving around until I saw a man. He didn't know but said, "Wait here." I did. He came back with another man who said, "Follow me." I said, "Praise God," and followed him. We wound around down one lane and then another and ended right at the door. I thanked him profusely; and parked in probably a foot of snow which was coming down very heavy by now. As I gathered all my material to get out I said, "Lord, please don't let me get stuck here." I didn't know how I would even back my car out if it kept snowing let alone get back down the mountain. I wasn't staying overnight, just speaking that morning.

The girls were wonderful, every one of them so excited about the snow and how great it was! I felt like a wimp as I kept

l that snow pile up and wondered what the Lord had
he finale'. The worship team sang prior to my message
the girls looking out those huge windows, asking the
the snow stop so I could get home. There was a bare
tree, with stark black branches just outside the window. The snow
was beginning to adorn these very small, brittle branches when all
of a sudden I looked, and there was a bird perched right there looking around as though it didn't have a care in this world. Well, you
know that Scripture, "…not a sparrow falls that I don't know about
– Fear not, then; you are of more value than many sparrows" (see
Matthew 10:29, 31).

You see how He helped my hinds' feet get traction again?
Not only that, He sent another bird and before I got up to speak He
had two of them out there, totally fearless in the snow. I could tell
I needed to either get my act together or live in shame. I was able
to weave some of what was happening into my message but I could
not tell you what the theme was I taught about. At the end I like to
have question and answer time and the girls' response was great.
We had a time of prayer and then they put me in a chair, surrounded
me and prayed for my safe journey home. What a precious group of
women, I don't think I shall ever forget them and I know I shall not
forget the journey to get to them.

After each trip is over I am exhilarated and flooded with joy.
The Lord has so many different ways to teach me how to keep on
climbing with the Hinds' feet He has given me. I know that each
lesson is necessary so that I learn not only to use my Hinds' feet but
to rely on them with confidence. I feel so blessed that He is taking
the time to teach me how to be 'fleet of foot' in this new arena.

Hinds' feet for Prayer

Our journey as widows is as varied as the gifts and talents
that the Lord gives to each of us. In sharing my journey with you I
pray there will be something of value for you to latch on to that will

help strengthen you in your journey.

Prayer for believers is not a gift, it is a command. I'm sure it isn't a news flash that Satan absolute hates it when a Christian reads the Bible or prays. He will fight us with everything at his disposal to keep us from doing either one. It truly takes hinds' feet (feet that cling with tenacity, and climb with exuberance those impossible heights,) to stay committed to prayer or to being in the Word, but what a blessing when we obey God and do that very thing.

All through my life the Lord had given me godly older women to teach me higher levels of prayer, so prayer is very much a part of my life. However, when Bill died there were times when all I could say was, "Jesus." I would walk in my back patio and just say over and over, "Jesus, Jesus." Just saying His name was enough. I don't want anyone to think she has to have long, eloquent prayers to be heard. Never! His name is enough.

Because the devil fights so ferociously to keep us from prayer, we need to ask the Lord for iron in our soul and a spirit of determination to keep us in prayer. I like to think of that little hind with feet that fly fearlessly over sheer rock places, and remember that the Lord told us that He would make our feet like hinds' feet so we can cling tenaciously to Jesus, and climb our high places of trouble with victory through Jesus, our Rock.

I belong to a very large church and yet our prayer groups are attended by very few. It helps to remember that the Lord didn't need a crowd, just two or three and there He was in the midst. I was asked to do a workshop on prayer at our Women's Retreat one spring. The theme was *God in the Midst of her Prayer*. When asked how many hand-outs I would need to be printed for the women, I said, "I think 150 would probably be over what we will have at the workshop." The dear friend who had asked, looked at me, and glibly said, "We'll print 200." I was thinking again of the small turn outs for the different prayer groups and breathed a prayer, *"Lord, please don't let these handouts be wasted."* You can see my lack of faith.

Our retreats are covered with an abundance of prayer for the speaker and all the workshops and certainly for all the women that the Lord was bringing. It was time for my workshop and I went up to the podium to prepare for the next hour. With five minutes to go there were probably fifty to sixty women sitting in the audience. I closed my eyes and prayed for them as I know our women want to learn how to pray, I know they are hungry for prayer. So I was grateful for this many. As I opened my eyes I could almost hear the Lord chuckling (does God chuckle?). It was like floodgates had opened. Three hundred women came and of course we ran out of handouts!

I believe even that was of the Lord. The women shared and laughed together and a bond was created right at the beginning. I used half my time to teach and the other half for the women to put into practice the teaching— to pray! I don't know when I have been so blessed. The prayer was like popcorn popping, women all over the room expressing their needs, their hurts, their longings and their hopes. The hour seemed like fifteen minutes and was over so soon. Many of the women came up afterwards to express how God had blessed them and opened a channel of prayer within them to flee to Him with *everything*! There were so many trials to go through in preparing for that workshop. I could almost hear the Lord saying, "That's why I'm making your feet like hinds' feet."

I just want to make a point here about when the Lord calls you to minister in your given area. Expect the trials, get excited about them (see James 1:2–4); God is in control, and we stand in the victory Jesus has won for us (see 1 Corinthians 15:57). If I'm speaking or doing a workshop, whatever I do, I am not surprised at the tests or trials that come. To me that is the Lord squeezing me out so there is only room for Him. Isn't that what we want?

Ask the Lord to make your feet like hinds' feet so that you can cling tenaciously to your Rock, Jesus! He is no respecter of persons, He has given all of us gifts and talents and He wants us to use them to display His mighty love and power. There is no greater pleasure than being used by the Lord, and as He gives us that amazing pleasure we can understand a bit better why we are widows at this time of our lives. He has a plan for us (see Jeremiah 29:11), and He has not forgotten us (see Isaiah 49:15). We can choose to cling to our grief or enter in with our whole being to be used freely by the God of the universe. It's our choice.

Hinds' Feet for Young Widows

A widow at any age has special problems and it is reassuring to know that the Lord has the answers for all of us. It seems to me we are having an increase in younger widows these days. Many still have children at home and sometimes finances are a very real problem. Younger widows can apply all that I have written but God wants to give them the hind's feet they need to be able to hurdle their problems of sufferings and responsibilities. There is financial help through social services. Let your church know you have needs, whatever kind they are. Our church has many programs of helps and I'm sure other churches do also.

I want to address re-marrying. There is such a danger here of jumping ahead of the Lord because of tremendous needs, for the children, for finances and for physical needs. There is a danger for older widows as well; this is a time when we need 'hinds' feet' to cling in *waiting* for the Lord to lead us. There is nothing wrong in remarrying, in fact the Lord says in 1st Timothy 5:14 that the younger widows should marry. The Apostle Paul also wrote, "Now to the unmarried and the widows I say: it is good for them to stay unmarried, just as I am. But if they can't control themselves, they should marry. It's better to marry than to burn with lust." (1 Corinthians 7:8)

We must always remember God *knows* we are widows; He has a plan for our lives and He also knows we are not all called to remain single. The important thing to remember if you choose to remarry is to wait for the *husband God has picked out for you*. I have counseled precious young widows who have run ahead of Him, positive that the man they married was from the Lord. Too many of them end up in disastrous situations. There is a need here to wait for clear leading of the Lord and seek the council of a pastor or someone else whose wisdom you respect.

Take your sexual appetites to the Lord in prayer. He is well able to curb those desires and make you strong to overcome. I was in my early sixties when Bill died, which certainly isn't like being in my 30's or 40's. Nevertheless, there are still sexual desires at that age. I remember going to the Lord and saying, "Father, You have to take these desires from me as Bill isn't here any longer and it certainly isn't Your will for me to indulge in immorality." He heard my plea and answered. Did I have to pray about this more than once? Yes. I kept praying until every temptation was gone. In today's culture sexual immorality is as common as breathing, but God's attitude toward it hasn't changed one bit. I recommend reading 1 Corinthians 6:16–20. If possible, read this passage in the Amplified Bible.

The devil loves to get us out of fellowship with the Lord, he laughs with glee when we are missing all the blessings the Lord has for us. And that is what happens when we are out of God's will. Keeping our eyes on Jesus is imperative for all of us. Here is a little reminder for that young widow with children: God loves your children more than you do. He promised to be a Father to the fatherless—and He is. Psalm 68:5 tells us, "A father to the fatherless, and a judge and protector of the widows, is God in His holy habitation" (Amp).

Church fellowship is so needful, not only to build us up in our faith, but also to allow fellow believers to help others in their time of need. Our church has a fellowship for widows and that is the place to make known your needs, to let others encourage you by prayer and loving you and your children. If there aren't any grandparents near, ask if one of the older women in the church wouldn't like to be a surrogate grandparent. Older people love being around youngsters so both generations benefit.

Don't forget that God is your invincible army, He will fight for you (see Habakkuk 3:19). Take your problems to Him, hold them up before Him and tell Him you trust Him to take care of your needs. Are bills overwhelming you? Spread them out on your bed and ask Him to give you the wisdom of what you should do with this *impossible* situation. Believe He hears you and believe He will answer you. The only stipulation God put on giving us all the wisdom we need is that we are to come *full of faith*, not with a divided mind. Can we say, "I believe You for this—but I'm not sure about that"? No, we are to trust Him for everything. His unfailing love is unfailing; don't ever forget how much He loves you and wants to bless you.

Ask the Lord to give you that friend He has picked out for you, one you can trust, pray with and depend upon to help you through the hard times. Above all, remember, that Jesus is the best Friend we will ever have.

Use your hinds' feet to keep climbing upward until you reach the goal the Lord has set for you. It will be magnificent.

Needing Hinds' Feet in time of Trouble and Suffering

There is a quote I want to share with you. This man lived from 1542 to 1591. He lived over four hundred years ago, and died when he was 49, yet he left a profound truth for us to discover and live by today.

> *"I am not made or unmade by*
> *the things which happen to me*
> *but by my reaction to them.*
> *That is all God cares about."*
> St. John of the Cross

Isn't that good, so simple, so true and so insightful? How am I reacting to the things which happen to me as a widow? Is God pleased with my trust in Him or am I floundering in my faith?

One thing most widows agree on, we feel we are prey for the mechanics and repairmen of the world! There have been many discussions among women regarding rude repairmen and exorbitant charges we are faced with if a husband, or man, isn't in evidence. Most of us have not only heard this we have experienced it! I remember that looking for a new car indeed turned out to be a time of trouble. Approaching the fourth car lot of that day, the salesman on duty looked at me with the same condescending attitude I had experienced all day. I stated at once what I wanted and the amount I could spend.

He wouldn't show me cars until we went into his office and he filled out lengthy forms. I explained numerous times I would not buy until I knew the price of his cars and what I would be allowed for trade-in for my car. Twenty minutes later he asked how I wanted to pay for the car. When he realized I meant what I had said, he glared at me, ripped the paper off his tablet with such hostility and so loudly that all the salesmen sitting at their desks in that room looked at me as if I was doing the abusing. My salesman then stood up and stalked off. I should have reported him but my embarrassment and distress were so great that I stumbled out of the office as quickly as possible, rushed to my car and broke into tears of humiliation.

I am going to quote in full, Exodus 22:22-24 from the Amplified Bible. Every widow needs to know the intensity of God's love for her.

"You shall not afflict any widow or fatherless child. If you afflict them in any way, and they cry at all to Me, I shall surely hear their cry; and My wrath shall burn; I will kill you with the sword, and your wives shall be widows and your children fatherless."

Wow! Do we ever have a defender and His name is God Almighty. Sitting in my car to upset to drive as yet (I couldn't see anyway because of my tears), I told the Lord I know He is my defense and He has heard this rude, abusive man. Now, I didn't ask God to kill him, but I said, "Lord, You are well able to take care of him!" I left the punishment part up to God.

It took those hinds' feet of cleaving to my Rock to persist in looking for a new car. I just wanted to crawl into a hole and forget the whole thing. The Lord saw my tears and discouragement and sent a dear friend of ours who helped me find the car the Lord had set apart just for me. He is so good.

There are different kinds of suffering such as physical, mental and emotional. My birthday and the anniversary of my husband's death are only a few days apart. These occasions seemed to almost always coincide with some heart-breaking event regarding relationships taking place in my family. All of this occurring simultaneously one year filled me with overwhelming grief. The Lord had steadily strengthened my faith in the four years since Bill had died, and I felt strong in that area. When these sad family events happened, I was surprised at how quickly my faith drained from me, like a tub of water when the plug is removed.

I knew doubt, discouragement and fear were used by the enemy to rob me of faith but I never knew grief could be used just as well. This was another kind of grief I was experiencing. The only parallel was that just as I couldn't stop my husband from dying, I also could not stop another human being from taking wrong paths; only God could do that. Love, listen and pray was all the Lord was asking me to do.

In trying to keep peace and accommodate the different personalities involved I felt like I had become a stomping rug for any and all pet peeves. No matter what I did, it wasn't right, it wasn't enough and nothing was being resolved.

I began to see a pattern while studying the life of David. God didn't set David up to defeat Goliath until David had learned to kill the bears and lions. My house and yard falling apart were my bears and lions, the relationships were my Goliaths. David wouldn't wear King Saul's armor. Instead, he chose his sling-shot. When he ran towards Goliath, he ran in the name of the Lord and for His glory, knowing God would give him the victory in this battle. I could picture David running and yelling at Goliath saying, "And all this assembly shall know that the Lord saves not with sword and spear; for *the battle is the Lord's* and He will give you into our hand" (1 Samuel 17:47 Amplified Bible. Emphasis mine.) .

In these relationship conflicts I "saw" myself trying to say the right thing, do the right thing, and be all *I was supposed to be; all of it* ending in abysmal failure with every effort. When all along the Lord was waiting patiently as if saying, *If you will get out of the way I will take care of this for you, for the battle is Mine!* With all this turmoil I desperately needed some time away to seek the Lord and His wisdom. When preparing to leave, I purposely didn't take my Bible as the hotel where I was going would have a Gideon Bible. Fresh, clean pages, without words highlighted and underlined. I needed to know what the Lord wanted me to do and discover His direction.

As I read the Old Testament passages, the Lord consistently encouraged me to trust His sovereignty in my life. He also caused me to see He was just as sovereign in the lives of those I was lifting up in prayer. I have this terrible habit of thinking my family's spirituality depends on me. What a relief to finally relinquish such a burden. As I pondered the reason why so many trials were needed for God to perfect me (I was convinced I was the worst sinner the Lord ever saved), He brought to my mind the fire that destroyed the condominium where my mother had once lived.

Mother's home was filled with antiques and many were lost in the fire. Her old secretary with its collector's china pieces was burned beyond repair. Even its glass doors had broken in the heat of the fire. The remaining charred shelves held plates, bowels and pitchers that were burned to a solid black, inside and out. As the black residue was removed we were amazed that not one piece of china was cracked, chipped or broken. I thought of how Dresden china is fired three times to burn the gold and colors on it permanently. We are told that God uses trials by fire to teach eternal values. I thought of the china that was man-made, yet had withstood the heat of a fire that destroyed a whole building without one piece of that china broken or cracked!

If man is capable of doing such amazing work with fire, how much more my heavenly Father wants to accomplish in me through fiery trials. He reminded me that my faith was more precious to Him than perishable gold (see 1 Peter 1:7). The Lord reaffirmed to me that no matter what the fiery trial should be, His love and wisdom is ever the answer

Returning home with fresh courage and I felt a better insight into God's plan and purpose for all of us I was ready for the healing to begin. Was there instantaneous success? No. It took several years of healing before that sweet bond of fellowship was restored. What amazed me so during these years of restoration was the change in *me*. When bumpy times came and the tendency to make me that rug began, I submitted all of it to the Lord.

In the past I would retaliate, with the *flesh* ruling supreme on both sides, and defeat was guaranteed once again. Now the Lord was showing me that if I would humble myself, and quit trying to fix the problem or defend myself, or trying to prove how right I was, He would take care of the problems—and He has. He was teaching me two important lessons through all this. I am not sure which lesson was first but I knew He didn't want me clinging closely to any relationship. He was to be First in my life, and He wanted me to learn that He was enough. I did and He is.

The other lesson is ongoing. Without my husband I had to make every decision, there weren't any options. The tendency is to allow the flesh to take over. Then pride creeps in, not the *I am great* kind of pride, but the *I can do it all* kind.

The Lord used the problems in relationships to show me, I truly can do nothing in myself. As I said, it's an ongoing lesson, but I am far enough along in that process to know how wonderful it is to just be able to say, "Here, Lord, take this and do what You want with it. You're my husband now." I learned that this is the *rest* that we are told not to fail to enter into (see Hebrews 4:11). I felt the Lord was speaking directly to me when He said that "he who has once entered (God's) rest also has ceased from the weariness and pain of human labors, just as God rested from those labors peculiarly His own" (Hebrews 4:10 AMP).

119

He taught me anew that all trials are needful. In His sovereignty He sends them so I might see from His viewpoint, grow in faith and trust more deeply in Him. It takes hinds' feet to climb back up the mountain of faith; my own feet slip, stumble and fall. But the Lord gives me hinds' feet so that I can make spiritual progress upon my high places (of trouble, suffering or responsibility)!"

God's Promises, God's Power
Our Choice

❖ When the obstacle facing me is so huge I can't see over it, around it or through it, will I remember my hinds' feet are for climbing the impossible heights?

❖ When faced with decisions, whether small or catastrophic, will I remember He already has the answer? And *knowing*, that if I will move forward, sure-footed (hinds' feet with faith), He will share His wisdom with me.

❖ Prayer is one of the most powerful tools the Lord has given us. When the enemy is saying, "You don't need this; you don't have time for prayer"; - will I put on my tenacious hinds' feet and refuse to stop praying?

Chapter Seven

My Ark of Triumph

You have always had an Ark, O God.
In Noah's day it was an ark of safety.
In Moses' day, the ark represented Your presence.
At the Cross You made Jesus Your Ark, (Romans 3:25-31)
giving me both safety and His presence.

Jesus - My Ark of Triumph

Man builds edifices to boast of mastery.
God clothes His victories with Christ's humility.

While visiting Paris, I became intrigued with the Arc de Triomphe that Napoleon had built to commemorate the triumphs of his Grande Armee`. It is an enormous monument with beautiful carvings depicting victory over different battles. The picture in front of this chapter was taken at the time of that visit.

I am aware that Arc de Triomphe in English is: Arch of Triumph; and of course, the monument itself is an arch. Standing before that renowned monument, realizing why it was built, meditating on how much Napoleon wanted to glorify his victories, caused me to have a new and even greater appreciation of my Lord Jesus Christ. I couldn't help but compare it with the Lord's triumph on the cross. The cross was ugly, unadorned, just two pieces of wood nailed together.

Napoleon had thousands of soldiers to gain his victories for France. Jesus won His victory over sin all alone and He won it for the whole world.

I thought of another similarity regarding the eternal flame that burns beneath the Arc for France's Unknown Soldier. The Lord's soldiers are not unknown to Him, our names are written in His Book of Life. We are also His trophies (see 2 Corinthians 2:14)! I am so grateful to be one of His trophies, aren't you? Every time I looked at that monument I was reminded of Jesus – my Ark! He is my Ark of safety, my Ark of victory. In my Ark, Jesus, there is all I will ever have need of.

Therefore, it seemed fitting to me that there should be a chapter in this book to proclaim His glorious triumphs, for the world and in my life.

"...He always leads us in triumph..."

Triumphing over Loneliness

I don't know who wrote the following definition of loneliness, but it is an accurate description of how we feel.

Loneliness is not simply a matter of being alone; loneliness is that feeling that nobody else truly cares what happens to you. Loneliness can be described as the feeling of not being meaningfully related to others.

Loneliness is the sense of being left out, isolated, estranged, abandoned, or not being understood. It may feel as if there is no one who is responsive to our deep hunger for support and caring. (Author unknown)

As I read all these feelings that come from loneliness, I can see where the Lord has filled every one of those needs! He is always with me just as He promised (see Hebrews 13:5). He has never left me.

I have been a widow for fifteen years and I can remember how I felt in the beginning of my widowhood. The description above fit me perfectly. Through all these years the Lord has consistently reminded me of Hebrews 13:5. In the Amplified Bible the phrase, "I will not leave you or forsake you," is so strong that it is repeated three times. I held on to the promise in that verse and said, "Okay, Lord, I believe You. Please take my loneliness away." When I still felt lonely I would ask the Lord to manifest Himself to me. Almost always He would respond, by a phone call, or someone just dropping by to say, "Hello," or those special times when He made His presence to me so very real.

I am so aware that the Lord is always with me and I cannot remember the last time I was lonely. Does that mean I don't miss Bill? Of course I miss him, but not with that terrible pain that I had in the beginning. I know I am going to be with him for eternity. God has a life for me here and now and that is what I am concentrating on until it is His time to take me home.

In the beginning when loneliness would try to creep in I would stop and remind myself that the Lord was right there with me. He promised He would never leave me and I know He won't. So I don't feel isolated or abandoned.

When trouble or oppression reared their ugly heads I would remind myself that He is my refuge and strength and *He was right there with me*. Trouble or oppression lead to a keen awareness that loved one is not with us and I would think of Psalm 46:1, 7, and 11 which says again and again He is our high tower of refuge. Because of the promises of His Word, and His faithfulness to fulfill them, I no longer had that deep hunger for support and someone to care for me. The Lord was my high tower of refuge and it was He who supported me.

I never see that promise without thinking of the round tower of Glendalough (pronounced "Glendalock") in Ireland. There are many towers all over Ireland but the one in Glendalough was built in the ninth century and was my favorite. It is 110 feet tall and was built by the monks to take refuge in when the Vikings devastated their valley. There is only one entrance with a safe inside stairway and no windows except at the very top from which they could see their enemies coming many miles away. When the Vikings attacked, the monks were able to rain down arrows or hot oil on them from those windows. The towers are built of stone so their enemies couldn't burn them out or shoot them with their arrows.

All of that is such a beautiful picture to me of Jesus. When the enemy of oppression attacks (which I think can lead to loneliness) I visualize that high tower, Jesus said He was my high tower and refuge, so I run to Him and let Him scatter all my enemies.

Where I live, high cost, destitution and desperation have already begun for many people. I know my only security is in the Lord, not in a pension or Social Security. Once more He promises to be my refuge and stronghold. A stronghold is a fortified place, a place of security. I love it when the Lord gives me such concrete promises to hang onto.

How do I know He will do all this? He says that for those who reverently fear and worship Him, He will establish His word and confirm His promise to them (see Psalm 119:38). And He has. He has never once failed me in fifteen years

I know I am quoting a lot of scripture, but I want you, my fellow sisters in grief, to realize that is what we have to cling to. His Word is Truth, even as He is Truth. He *will* do what He has promised for us. Our part is to *believe* Him. When the pangs of loneliness start, run to Him, and remind yourself that He promised to never, no never, no never, leave you or forsake you. He carries you with Him in His triumph over every enemy, even that culprit loneliness!

The Blessings of His Triumph

I want to share some of the blessings the Lord has given me. I am always so humbled to think the Lord could use me, remembering always that it is not I but Christ. (See Galatians 2:20)

And, please, remember He wants to use you. For many of you I'm sure He already has. But for those who feel the Lord could never use you, that's a great place to be, a good attitude to have! The more we feel He could never use us, the more He is able to use us. He told Paul that His strength is made perfect in our weakness. When you are weak then you are strong in His strength (see 2 Corinthians 12:9, 10).

I have already shared that when Bill died I asked the Lord to use me or take me home. I didn't want to stay here and spin my wheels. Little by little in the months and years ahead the Lord would use me. As I learned the lessons He was sending, He increased the responsibilities of the ministries He wanted me involved in.

When I was thirty I read 2 Timothy 1:7 and took it for my life verse. "For God has not given us the spirit of fear, but of power and of love and a sound mind" (KJV). I loved that verse and as you have read my story you can see how I needed to know fear wasn't from God, but power, love and a sound mind were!

Someone once told me the words *fear not* appear 365 times in the Bible. I think I found 64 or 65 of them. These were so important to me I wrote a little booklet about the *Fear Not's of God*. In the chapter on Hinds' Feet in this book, I shared how the Lord let me teach about *fear not*. He did the same with little prayer booklets I had written. I never dreamed the Lord would have me share all this with His daughters' years later. It was all progressive responsibility, but oh, so gratifying to be used by Him.

The tremendous love and concern I have for our women is from Him, any gifts and abilities are all from Him. I have thoroughly learned that in myself I can do nothing! Someone recently asked me if I still became nervous before I speak, and I said, "You bet!" It is when I begin to give the message the Lord has given me that the excitement comes. I want to see changed lives that will bring glory to the Lord. Our women want that too, so we work together.

His gifts and calling are irrevocable. When He gives them, He never takes them back (see Romans 11:29). The Bible tells us that the Holy Spirit gives gifts to each of us individually, just as He wills. The Lord wants us using those gifts freely wherever He takes us. He showers His blessings on us so abundantly and He expects us to scatter these amazing benefits just as lavishly. I am firmly convinced that our imaginations could not begin to comprehend the abundance God wants to bestow upon us and through us to others. I visualize a banquet table heaped beyond measure with all the wealth of heaven. We come begging to a generous God for peace, for patience, and for deliverance from envy, despair, jealousy, and unforgiveness, when all the time God says, "Take, eat; my Son has provided all you will ever need."

What does it take to make all that is on that banqueting table mine? *Faith.* Do we actually believe He will take our loneliness and fill it with new companionships or something else equally worthy in His wisdom for us? Do we trust Him without those niggling little doubts that like to creep in, about finances, health, guidance, and above all, about the new life He has planned for us? Our Lord Jesus said, "I came that they may have and enjoy life, and have it in abundance (to the full, till it overflows)" (John 10:10b Amplified Bible).

Enjoy life, have it in abundance, overflow with it? That concept might be too far out there when we are new widows and in pain. The beautiful part of the Word of God is that it isn't a concept, it is *truth*. Here is where we engage in faith and say, "Lord, I don't feel joy, I don't see abundance in my life. Nevertheless, I choose to believe Your Word, so will You please work this truth into my life." He is triumphant in every area of our lives; He has already given us that abundant life and our part is to *wait in faith* while He works in us to bring it about.

The promises we are given sound wonderful, but in the newness of widowhood we don't see or feel any of them. Nevertheless, they are already ours. The fact is that He is our heavenly husband, He chooses to never leave or forsake us, and He has made Himself always available to us. All these things show an overflowing abundance of His blessings towards us. It's a foretaste of the abundant new life He already has planned for each one of us. Does all this mean we will never have trials, troubles or heartache again? No, but it does mean that we will triumph in whatever we face as His blessings include wisdom, strength, love, whatever the trial we are in requires. In the next section we learn He even fights our battles for us; no wonder we cannot lose!

Triumphant in Every Battle

How are we able to triumph in every battle? Because as the Lord told us, "Do not be afraid nor dismayed because of this great multitude, for *the battle is not yours, but God's*" (2 Chronicles 20:15, emphasis mine).

The battle of keeping a house and yard together without my husband was very real; there are always many needed repairs to be made. I had to learn to trust God for the right people and get out of the way so He could fight these battles for me. I know most widows go though all the above and it is a painful learning procedure. My problem was with my mind. I was always thinking if I did this, or that, or called this one or that one, then all would be well. And of course, it wasn't. The Lord let me spin my wheels until I was exhausted. Then I would moan, "Lord, You just have to *do* something!" Only God could have the patience needed for someone like me. When I stopped trying to do it myself and turned it over to Him, it was taken care of.

Every battle I encountered was divinely appointed by the Lord to build my faith. With each conflict I knew I had a choice. If I chose fear, that would bring dishonor to the Lord; if I chose to trust Him I could almost hear the joy bells in heaven ringing!

There were times in the battle of relationships that the fighting was fierce. I had to release every thought, fear and anxiety to the Lord, and once more proclaim by faith that I *knew* He was fighting for me. Peace never failed to fill me when I would stop trying in my own strength and relinquish every bit of the battle to the Lord.

Again, in my own mind I would devise ways to circumvent the enemy. In the physical, I would place barriers to defeat those who would come against me. For instance, monitoring phone calls and not answering if I knew that person calling would probably hurt me again. I tried not being home or available to avoid confrontational people. I wasn't able to handle these types of people and when I was forced to be around them I would usually keep a tight grip on my emotions until I was home alone and then I would fall apart. But the Lord kept the pressure on me by not letting those unsavory people stop in their pursuit to reach me. You can see I didn't have a great Christian attitude. I finally saw my wisdom was foolishness and the physical barriers were an exercise in futility.

When every vestige of my own self-centered endeavors was given to Him, when confession of my very uncharitable heart was made, and the entire problem given to the Lord, *then* He was able to fight my battle. How did He do that? In this instance He changed my heart *first*, and then He changed other's hearts. Healing and restoration was the wonderful triumph.

Sometimes the battle is in the mind such as when hard decisions have to be made, and there is no husband to talk them over with, or the panic that hits when the crisis situations happens. For me it was a blocked garbage disposal with a houseful of guests coming the next day for Thanksgiving! Another time my garage door fell off with no way to lift it to get my car out for an important meeting that was scheduled and no way to secure the garage from intruders. I could fill this page with the thoughts that were crashing through my brain at all the possible catastrophes that would happen when both these battles appeared in my life. I remember saying, "Lord! You promised to fight for me, tell me what in the world I am going to do!"

Ever so softly the Lord said, "Call your son." Every widow knows that we don't like to bother our children as there is *so much* that goes wrong *all the time*. The garbage disposal chose to go out the night before Thanksgiving and I couldn't find a plumber, so I called my son. He came and thank God was able to fix the problem. With the garage door, it was daylight, and my son sent two of his men out to fix the problem for me. I am blessed with a wonderful son who has been so helpful so very many times. I have an equally wonderful daughter; she and her husband just happen to live out of town, so her brother gets the first call.

You might ask, "How is this God fighting your battles for you? It sounds more like your son fought the battles."

My son was God's *provision* for me and I can promise you most emphatically that if one of your children is not able to help you, the Lord *will have* that provision for you. You are so dear to Him and He is ever mindful of your needs and mine. We have such a wonderful, loving God, who cares about every detail of our lives, and who runs to fight our battles for us.

Isn't it wonderful, in that time of trouble, to know however bad it looks you are already triumphant because your God fights for you, victoriously.

Triumphant over Perilous Days

In the fifteen years Bill has been gone, wickedness has increased at an unprecedented rate. The Lord told us we should understand this, that in the last days there will set in perilous times of great stress and trouble hard to deal with and hard to bear (see 2 Timothy 3:1).

For those of us who are widows and many of us live alone we need to remember that the Lord is our refuge and high tower. "He is a refuge and stronghold in times of trouble (high cost, destitution and desperation)" (Psalm 9:9 AMP).

I have always thought that was such a perfect verse for the End Days we live in. The Lord's coming is soon and He is getting us ready to be with Him. We all want to live triumphantly in perilous times and the only way we can do that is stay in that abiding place with our Lord Jesus.

Earthquakes are frequent in Southern California and can be perilous. The minute I feel an earthquake coming I start praying as hard and fast as I can, "Lord! You are my shield!" I continue praying that until the quaking quits.

One night in the past year when we had had a pretty good shake I lay on my bed asking the Lord how I should pray for *the big one* we keep hearing is coming. I didn't hear anything but impressions began to come to my mind. The words, "Jesus is my Rock," played over and over in my mind. I saw Him as immovable, stable. I said, "Lord, You are my Rock, I choose to set my house on You. When an earthquake comes I believe You to keep my house together because You are my Rock, my foundation, and this house is Yours." With that I had peace about the *big one*. I pray this might help and encourage you. I don't know what will happen but I do *know* my trust is in Him and I know beyond a shadow of a doubt that nothing will happen to this house that isn't in His perfect will.

With the high cost of living today finances can be perilous for the widow. In the little group that I meet with we share on where to find that honest mechanic, (we now have a total of two we can trust,) honest plumbers, handymen, and so on. We also share information of where or how to get financial help. For instance almost all the utility companies have special plans for those whose incomes are below a certain level. If yours is, take advantage of that.

For our young widows with babies or toddlers who are really pressed for money, there are several areas of help through social services. I am thinking of WIC (The Special Supplemental Nutrition Program for Women, Infants and Children) that helps mothers buy milk and food for their babies. Depending on the income of the mother they can also help with rent.

For those who have a home paid for or some equity there is a reverse mortgage plan. You have to be 65 to qualify but it's a great plan as there are no payments. You can take a monthly supplement or draw larger sums out when needed for those crises that hit unexpectedly. When the person dies the heirs pay back the money that was used. Above all if there is a financial need *pray* and ask the Lord to show you His way to take care of that situation.

If you are not in a group or fellowship with other widows I strongly recommend that you find one. If you cannot find one, start one yourself, it is a precious time of fellowship of loving, praying and encouraging one another.

How can we be triumphant when our health fails? I urge you to read any of Amy Carmichael's books. What a woman of God she was and what amazing things she accomplished from her bed. She is an inspiration to any who reads of her life. God knows when we are ill, He knows the purpose He has in that, ask Him what it is.

I have heard women say, "Well, I don't have any gifts or talents; all I can do is pray." That always astounds me; there is nothing greater than prayer! I have been in prayer groups these past forty years and I can tell you from personal experience that without prayer my gifts and talents would never have been used to the extent God has used them with prayer.

And, we *all* have gifts from the Holy Spirit; the Bible tells us that we do (see 1 Corinthians 12:11). If you haven't discovered what yours are, get excited about them and ask the Lord to show you.

I want to close this section with Colossians 2:15, I love this verse!

"God disarmed the principalities and powers ranged against us and made a bold display and public example of them, in triumphing over them in Him and in it (the cross)." (Colossians 2:15 Amplified Bible).

Do you believe that? If yes, then shout "Hallelujah!" with me. Jesus has conquered every foe for you and me so we can walk in His victory.

Triumphing in Every Day Life

If you have ever been to a meeting of widows you know there is usually a box of tissues sitting nearby. As new women join the group and tell of the loss of their husband the tears flow. At the close of one of our monthly meetings our leader asked that we would look for things in the next month that brought joy to our hearts, write them down, and share at our next meeting.

What a great assignment! I wish everyone could have been there at that next meeting, the joy and laughter that came forth was wonderful. It was a much-needed project. It caused us to be on the lookout all month for those things that bring joy to our hearts.

The Lord has given me such joy in the triumphs He has brought in my life through adversity that I want to share a couple of these experiences with you. I really don't call them experiences; I call them adventures with the Lord!

I mentioned earlier in the book about borrowing my son's laptop and taking off. What I didn't mention was what happened *before* I got to my destination.

I was staying six days so I had packed my car with a suitcase, couple of tote bags, laptop and a purse the size of a tote bag. Early that morning I backed my car out of the driveway into the street, with my wheels still turned, my car died. I was in the middle of the street, couldn't turn my wheels to push my car to the curb, it was dead.

I sat there not believing for a minute what had happened. I reminded the Lord I had prayed about this trip, felt I was to go. Nothing. Thank God for cell phones as my car was definitely a danger zone. I called the Automobile Club for help and told the man my problem. He asked if I thought he should send a regular truck or a tow truck. Looking at my poor dead car, I said, "Probably a tow truck." There wasn't even a click, click, when I turned the ignition key on.

In the meantime I was frantically calling my son repeatedly, with no answer. I called on his cell, his home phone, nothing. That *never* happens, he always answers at one or the other. Then, I started calling my daughter; remember she lives much farther from me. Same thing, no one answered. My thinking was that one of them could drive me to my destination after my car was taken to the mechanic. I had reservations that took a three-day prior cancellation notice. The Lord didn't let me reach anyone but the Automobile Club.

After giving directions to the driver of the tow truck on where to take my car, I unloaded my very loaded car and hauled everything back in the house. Still trying to reach my children which I never did, at three that afternoon I called my dear friends who had reservations for the next night where I was staying, I told them my woes and asked for a ride the next morning with them. I was set to go, but a day late. I reached my daughter that evening and explained what had happened and as she was coming out to stay with me my last night she would take me back to the mechanic where my repaired car would be waiting for me. Early the next morning I called the mechanic and told him what had happened to my car. This is one of our honest mechanics so knew I could trust him.

I told the Lord the day before that I didn't know or understand what was going on but I trusted Him and believed He had a purpose. Even in not knowing why of all this happened, I was filled with peace. I was already praising the Lord that my car died at the end of my driveway. I could have been on the freeway, in the desert, anywhere on my way. I just have to enumerate the many ways the Lord blessed this newest adventure with Him.

1. The Lord graciously let this happen while I'm home.
2. He provided all the transportation I needed.
3. The hotel did not charge for that night I missed!
4. I was able to get a whole chapter written for this book while there, which I never would have, had I had my car, as I love to shop where I was staying. (That was probably why it happened!)
5. I called shuttle service when I wanted to go eat and got to share the Lord with a nice driver from New York.

My heavenly husband the Lord knows me so well. He knew my generator on the car was going out, the battery was dying, and He also knew if I was ever going to finish this book He needed to curtail my flitting here and there. Isn't He wonderful?

My second adventure I want to share with you is a bit more exciting and leans towards the traumatic. If I put a title on this I would call it, Triumphing in Adversity or What an Awesome, Amazing God We Serve.

I remembered what Corrie ten Boom said so often, "God doesn't have problems, He has plans."

I also want to say that year the verses the Lord had given me were Psalm 59:16-17, and one line in those verses was, "…You have been my refuge, a place of safety in the day of distress…" (Psalm 59:16 NLT) You will see how I needed that promise.

My daughter and I were coming home from Arizona and a storm had been predicted for the desert area. It was very gloomy and overcast but a great day for driving. I love to drive and isn't that a good thing as most of my adventures seem to take place in my car?

We reached Barstow and the weather began to show signs of the storm, starting with light little sprinkles; nothing serious. My daughter and I had prayed for journey mercies before we left so I *believed* the Lord for journey mercies.

As we approached Cajon Pass the sky opened up and we were deluged with rain. Then the white-out began. Immediately two words came to my mind as a question – peace or panic? I said, "Lord, I choose Your peace." The man in front of me did not turn his lights on so the only time I could see him was when he hit his brakes and two little red lights appeared.

Visibility was terrible and we were packed in with cars in all four lanes. However, I commented three different times to my daughter how sane everyone was driving for California drivers! I was praising the Lord for that. No one was trying to cut in or go fast, we were bumper to bumper trying to see. We looked like little ghost bundles huddled together trusting one another to stay in their own lane, lanes we could not see! I remember praying, "Lord, please help us to stay in our own lanes."

Even as I turned my windshield wipers to a fast speed because of torrential rain, the rubber blade began to creep out from the metal holder. I prayed out loud and asked the Lord to please control the blade as He knew there was no way I could do anything about it. Between the rain and white out vision was terrible so *I really needed my wipers to work*! The rubber blade just crept out more and more.

I reminded myself of my verse and prayed out loud, *"...Lord, You are my refuge, a place of safety in my day of distress..."* I continued praying, "Lord, You know I am in that place of distress right now. I thank You for the peace You have given me, but Lord take notice of that wiper blade – please, *You said* that You are my place of safety!"

We were probably about three-quarters of the way down Cajon and my wiper blade was coming clear around and slapping my side window. I could see through about one third of the window. On my daughter's side the wiper worked perfectly and she had vision through the whole window. God could have reversed that but I realized the test was for me. I was thinking it wouldn't do any good to stop at a gas station when we got to San Bernardino as they couldn't carry wiper blades for every car. Somehow the Lord had to get me home.

I prayed, "Lord, It isn't hard for You to stop the rain. You have to do something for me as I am putting my trust in You. Give me a pocket of dry weather just to get home." The white-out had finally lifted but not the rain.

I knew I was going to lose my blade any minute and said, "Lord, I expect You to *do* something." At the foot of the Cajon Pass the rain *stopped*, I shouted "Hallelujah!" I firmly believe one more swipe of my blade and it would have been flying in the wind. I had dry weather all the way home. We got my daughter's things transferred to her car and she headed for home. I jumped back in my car, headed for the auto parts store and had two new windshield wipers installed. It began to rain again as I returned home.

After that adventure I wrote in my journal, "Lord, this is praise to You for Your faithfulness to me always! I love You, love You, love You. Thank You for Your everlasting faithfulness to me and Your unfailing love. O my God, I put my trust in You."

During this time I seemed to hear Him say, "I never promised you a rose-covered path, I did promise I would never leave you or forsake you" (see Hebrews 13:5). And He never has; instead *He leads me always to triumph in Christ.*

We Triumph Always Because – His Banner Over Us Is Love

He brought me to the banqueting house and His banner over me was love (for love waved as a protecting and comforting banner over my head when I was near Him).
(Song of Solomon 2:4 Amp.)

There is no more perfect verse than the above to end this book, for the Lord does wave His banner of love over us through every trial, test and circumstance that invades our lives. He brings us to His banqueting house so that we might partake of His abundance freely.

He intervenes in the fierce wind storms as the enemy tries to blow us off course. He holds us close in the pain and agony of the first years of widowhood; and guides us, one day at a time, through the obscurity and confusion of the years ahead.

Pondering these past years, I see the eternal reason for all the tests and trials that the loss of a spouse brings. Everything that happens is to deepen and expand our faith in the Lord. In the Song of Solomon scripture above the key to all His blessings is "…when I was near Him." That's our part: to stay near Him, to abide in Him, to trust Him with our whole hearts; to believe His promises so that He is free to shower us with His blessings.

There is no way to stress the vital importance of staying in His word. When we do, we *know* Him more and more, and we also give Him the opportunity to reveal a word or promise He has that is personally ours and wants us to make claim to.

Widowhood is indeed a definitive turning point in the lives of widows (and widowers). Our lives have been changed forever but isn't it wonderful to know that the Lord is in total control of that change?

He loves us with an everlasting love; therefore, with cords of love He has drawn us to Himself. (see Jeremiah 31:3) Revel in His love, rest in His love. He is in full control of our lives, nothing surprises Him – settle down into His great love for you and know that His plan for your new life is *perfect* for you.

As widows we walk with our heavenly Husband in His unlimited triumph. Let us sing with the Psalmist who said in Psalm 47:1, "O clap your hands, all you people!

Shout to God with the voice of triumph and songs of joy!"

God's Promises, God's Power
Our Choice

Picture the Creator of the Universe rooting for you, saying over and over,

"Come on, you are a winner!" "You are triumphant over every battle, every pain, every problem, because I have fought and won the victory for you!"

You are triumphant over –
- ❖ Loneliness
- ❖ Every obstacle
- ❖ Perilous days
- ❖ Every day life and circumstances

Will we believe Him and trust in Him?
That is our challenge.

There may be someone reading this book who has never asked the Lord Jesus Christ to be your savior. The little prayer that follows is just for you. His love is unfailing and He wants you with Him for all eternity.

Prayer: Dear Lord Jesus, please forgive me of my sin.
I take you at your Word that you forgive those who ask.
Be my Lord, as You are my Savior. I give my self to
you. I'm yours. Thank you for being faithful and
saving me. I've asked and believe that you have saved me.
Amen.

Ask the Lord to help you find a Bible believing church and make yourself a part of that wonderful fellowship.

Afterwards

The following information was taken from the Net which I thought might be of interest to you. Widows are part of an enormous group of people and that number is growing as you can see by the information below.

The phrases, *redefining their lives…, and, just taking another approach to your "old" life*, are the world's way of dealing with the new life ahead of us. How blessed we are to know Jesus and realize He planned ahead for us and has that new life all ready. There are some good insights here that give us a better understanding of the world around us and perhaps show us a way the Lord can use us to help.

The Social Security Administration projects that by 2010, nearly 1,050,000 Americans will lose spouses each year, and by 2030 that number is expected to grow to more than 1.5 million. Those left behind face redefining their lives to deal in new ways with family and friends, as well as unresolved feelings and regrets left over from marriage. As many widowed Americans are finding, building a new life or finding new meaning sometimes requires just taking another approach to your "old" life.

Most widows — 69 percent — are women. And the numbers play havoc with the image of the frail, elderly widow. According to the National Vital Statistics Report, there are currently 500,000 widows under the age of 45 in the United States, many with children, leading to more complex issues.

Men who are widowed face a different set of stresses, proven by their death rate, which is three times higher than that for women in the same circumstances, according to the AARP.

Typically, men have two things working against healing: They don't expect to live longer than their wives, and their socialization and training tell them that they should be strong and silent. Often they have lost the only person in the world to whom they are comfortable confiding their feelings at a time when it is critically important to have someone to talk to.

We are in a new day where women are taking on more stressful jobs that may be contributing to increase in widowers.